Dot's Dateline

By: Dottie Zimmerman

1stBooks – rev. 1/22/02

Dot's Dateline

Dot's now going on 90 years young. She's lived alot longer than many and in those many years of life she's experienced much. One of her experiences was that of suddenly becoming a single female when her mate died. She was 65 years of age when her husband died. She waited awhile but she at last realized she still had alot of life left in her and she wanted to find another husband to share the rest of her life with. She tried to find this new husband through the newspaper 's singles want-ads. On these following pages are some of the letters which she received over the years. These upcoming letters will be kn own as "Dot's Dateline".

Hello- Thank you for your letter. Hope that you are well and happy. Weather here has turned cooler - a rest from the heat of August and early September. Fall will soon be in full swing. I'm a white male 5'8" , 190lbs. , salt and pepper hair, mustache. I'm not yet retired, hope this doesn't make a difference with you. You stated you were young and that's all that really counts. I'd love photos of you and what you enjoy. Have you visited Nashville? Would you like to visit? Are you a Florida native? Well, I'll close for now. Hope you will respond.   worthwhile, Lamar, (TN.)

Hello- Trust that you are well and happy. Hope that this address is correct. Your address was in Finder's Keepers from Iowa. It also states you enjoyed scenic drives and travel. I currently live outside Nashville, Tn.. When you have time I'd love to hear from you.
Best Wishes, Lamar (TN.)

Dear Dorothy, Hello sweetie. I want to thank you for replying to my ad in the Globe with such a nice and informative letter. Also I appreciate you sending the picture because I find you to be a very attractive and also a very desircable looking lady. Everything you said in your letter sure sounded good to me. Also I am a Scorpio. Also from your picture I can tell that you have a very good shape. Your letter to me was a long time getting to me from the time that I mailed it in to the Globe. In the meantime, I have met someone that likes me as much as I do her, and we have made committments to each other. I do not smoke or use drugs. I do drink some, but not very much. I am fully retired, almost 69 years of age, not wealthy but live very comfortable on my income. I have my own modern 3 bedroom house. As I said your letter was a long time getting here, if it had been received sooner, things could have possibly been a lot different. If things work out for me the way we hope that they will, then you will not hear from me anymore, but in the event they do not, then I would like to contact you again, of course, with your permission. So until then, I want to wish you the very best of everything. I enclose your picture.

Best Regards, Marvin (Florida)

Dear Dorothy, 5-3-91 received your letter and photo yesterday. The Examiner must forward all the replies at one time so I'm sorry I haven't answered sooner. I lived in St. Pete for over four years and just had to move away because of the humidity. Too bad I didn't get a chance to meet you then because I believe you would have made an excellent and passionate lover. Right? Take good care and don't give up.

Sincerely, Bill (AZ.)

2-21-90 Dear Dottie, Your reply to me was dated Dec. 1,1989 but I just received it today. Somebody goofed. I like your picture it's a sexy one. You're older than me. I'm 62 now as of 1-31 (born in 1928). I must ask this do you still enjoy sex? I do very much so and am extra large in that department (10 and a half inches). Your personality sounds nice and your face seems to be very pleasant. If this letter is not too late please write and tell me more about yourself. Ask me any question you like. Be frank and honest, as I am.

Sincerely, Bill (Fl.)

11-19-89 Dear Dottie, I have your name from a singles club and write to you because I like your description and living in Florida. I am a white retired sea captain, veteran of WW2, 5'5", 161 lbs.,76, well built and healthy. Don't smoke or use drugs. No dependants or pets. I am a widower live alone in my city house on a nice street. Have no money problems. I seek a gal to relocate to my place. She could hav e a nice home and be well respected. We call it sharing. I have an article on it from my November issue of AARP'S bulletin it's for elderly people like us who get lonesome living alone.Please answer. Thank you as ever. Bob (Fl.)

6-4-90   Dear Dottie,   What can I say? except I sure like the looks of your photo and the sound of your ad. You are a very sexy looking 77 year young lady. (followed by a picture of a happy face.)   If you are real respond with another photo a dn phone number to this s/w/m, 6'2', 170 lbs. 57 year young today.   Tell me more.   Looking   J.K. (AZ.)

6-5-90   Dear Dottie,   Thank you very much for your reply to my ad in the Globe. I received so many replies that it is not possible to establish contact with all.   However think that it is only fair to send a thank you to every one who took the time and effort to reply.   Thanks again and best of good fortune to you in your search for a companion. Sincerely H.H.(MO.)

1-23-90   Hi Good Looking,   Received your nice letter and photo today. It sure takes a long time for them to mail your letter out after they receive it from you. Anyway, you sound interesting wish you lived closer to me at least you are in Fla.. I feel flattered getting a letter from a woman so much younger than myself. The trend today is older women are looking for younger men and I can understand why a woman never gets too old to perform a normal sex life but a man does. As far as myself I have an open mind when it comes to sex. I'm sure you know what I mean.   I like it that you are a social drinker. I am retired from the Ford Motor Company in Dearborn Michigan in 1967 and went to the Florida Keys lived there for 14 years. Have been in central Florida since. I now live in a mobile home here in the Ocala National forest about 20 miles east of Ocala. I live all alone have female visitors around for awhile. I am old in years but young in mind when it comes to women. I am clean type of guy shower and shav e everyday. I don't care to travel to much . I would like to meet an open minded aggressive woman that living and let live. She is on the wild side and that is just great. I don't believe in a jealous relationship. I want a fun type woman.

I am sending you a photo made last Thanksgiving it will give you an idea of what I look like, I'm sure you can't expect too much from an 87 year old man.

A little more about my past. I was born in Kentucky in a farm taught school for two years. Went to Michigan in 1925 worked at Ford Motor Co. for over 42 years. Had a good job there was on salary.   Was an engineer and supervisor for the main office buildings there.

If you write again feel free to ask me any questions you wish and don't be shy say what you please and let it all hang out. Feel free to be as outspoken as you wish.   all for now,   hugs and kisses,   Tommy (Fl.)

This next one was sent in the form of a greeting card. On the front there is a teddy bear relaxing on a folding chair on the beach. The fron reads   Dorothy even though you're there in Sarasota and I'm here in Pittsburgh, I still feel close to you.   (this is what is inside the card) Hi Dorothy, Loved your letter and picture. If you like the pictures I've enclosed why not give me a call. (then there is a heart hand drawn with his name in the center)   (the bottom on the card is printed and it reads) That's because will all our shared memories,all our hopes and dreams and all our love... We're never really far from each other.   THINKING OF YOU DON

This next letter is from Dot to the potential gentleman friend. 11-23-88 Hi Honey,After reading your ad in the Globe I decided to write. My birthdate is May 9,1912. My sun sign is Taurus. I have been a widow for ten years. Relocated here from Collingdale, Pa. near Philadelphia , Pa. . Wanted a change from the cold weather and Sarasota is my kind of climate. I live with my son in his home. I am 5'7" tall, 120 lbs.. Haven't met the man of my dreams yet, maybe yo are him. If you answer I'll write more next time.   Sweet Dreams Dottie"Please send me a picture of yourself"

This was the response.3-27-89Hi Dottie,I'm Frank. I am unable to explain it, but only received your letter and three others on Friday Marcdh 24, and all of them were dated about the same time as yours Nov. 23,1988. So what hapened to them for four months I don't know. Anyway, it was real nice of you to answer.

I'm single, live alone in a non-luxury condo in a retirement community about three miles north of airport. Lived here about 15 months and have been making a number of improvements and replacements. (almost finished)

Also come from Delaware County in the Media area, near Granate Run Mall which is on Baltimore Pike. But lived and worked in Delaware for 33 years.

So if you are still free, please drop me a line and the best time to call you and maybe we can meet for lunch. Am returning your letter only if you forgot what you wrote. You can return it to me. Take care.

Sincerely, Frank (Fl.)

4-8-89Dear Dottie,Received your name and address from "Friendly Singles Club" and would like to get to know you. This is of course all up to you as I am 20 years younger than you. I do hope to retire from tele. co. in about two years...you look like a fun person to be with as I too like all kinds of fun. Like to travel and have a nice looking woman at my side, as you seem to be! The photo is kind of dard so I couldn't see much except your nice looking legs. I am seeking unity of two people, in mind, body and glands, hoping to develop similiar goals and complimenting each other with achieving those goals, I want someone who will give me emotional support as well as physical release! Now it's your turn to write to me and let me know if you concur, my name is Jerome , 57, will be 58 May 3,1989, 6'2", 230lbs. and am enclosing a photo for you to keep. Could you send me one of yours? P.S. Call me Jerry as you are my new friend to be! If you feel that I might be too young for you please keep in mind I will find my older woman girlfriend, one who will be happy and contented and if you think that you cannot express your desire, wants and needs to me, let me assure you that I can bring out all the youthfulness you have locked up in your beautiful body! and all that you thought you'd never experience again! Write me a letter, let us correspond exchanging view points, photos and let's see what happens - O.K.? Can you wear 3" heels so we can dance cheek to cheek?

Sincerely yours, I am Jerry (N.J.)

S.F. Bay area, visited friends and talked at more AA groups. Also, talked at a couple in TX.

Weather was lovely. Ran into rain in Kingmon, AZ. and at Barstow, CA..

No problem with diabetes. Check every 3 or 4 days and blood sugar is normal. I hope the stock market stabalizes and soon. I'm too old and comfortable to go through another like the 30's. How about you?

My two children and grandaughters were at lake before I left. Also, my good fishing buddy and AA friend was down. We caught a fin bass only one real good one.

I stayed here with my neice last year. She has her son here now. I have an apt I've rented and will move into Sunday the 15th.. Will still use this address though.

I intend to stay in Los Vegas until middle of February, then return home via. Los Angeles when I will visit my son.

I have an appointment at VA. eye clinic in K.C. on March 7th.. I plan to be there on 6th. for my grandaughter's 6th. birthday.

I would like to meet you. I too, feel as if I knew you.

Maybe, you will decide to come and visit me in the Azores, this spring, or summer - write - LoveChuck (N.V.)

1-24-88Hi Dottie,Thanks for answering my ad. Wish we could have seen the new year in together too. I like your picture very pretty looking and sexy looking gal.

I'm a Taurus too I guess April 24,1918. I am of French decent. I don't pay too much attention to signs. Just never got into it.

I'm retired from a local furniture store, where I was employed as credit manager for 26 years . I lost my wife of 33 years in April of 86 after a long illness (heart trouble and emphasema). Don't think I spelled that right but you know what I mean.

I gave all my statistics in the ad. Except, I have blue eyes and white hair.

Have just recently sold my home and purchased a new mobile home. I'm not rich either Dottie but am comfortable. You would find me easy to get along with, good snese of humor, incurable romantic and can do my part in making the sparks fly. I'm honest, thoughtful, tender and kind.

Dottie, I'm going to be at my son's home in St. Pete for a week or so as of next Sunday. Why don't you write me there and mazybe we can meet some place . write.Max (FL.)

I don't go to singles bars or clubs. Scared of all the diseases around today. Well, I'll hush for now, pretty lady, by the way, you say you will send me a better picture if I answer your letter. You must be kidding but go ahead and prove it. If you write me in St. Pete, give me your phone number. Sure hope we can get together. We didn't get to celebrate new years eve but the year is just beginning honey.

I live in the north west part of the state, near the Gulf . Came from Michigan 30 years ago. Live close to Panama City, snow white beaches.

More later. Please Write.

Love, Max

p.s. Would love to have a letter from you, waiting for me in St. Pete.

pps. Picture was taken while a friend and I were fishing on the river last September.

9-3-88My dear Dottie:When God scattered stars into space, he planned treasures for us to discover, like love, life and people like you.

The description you depict of yourself, along with your photo, describes in essence, if not in total, the vintage of womanhood I am seeking. I would be richly blessed, if the winds of chance brought us together, and I were the one to love and be loved by one such as you. As in our September years, when our years are a precious few let us make them our Golden Years, the very,very best of our lives. Was it not Robert Browning who wrote: "Come grow old with me, the best is yet to be, the last of life for which the first was made." He also wrote: "Life, without love is but a tomb".

Your photo overwhelmes me. You are most striking in your womanly beauty, and you being 5' 7", weighing 120 pounds puts me in a state of ecstasy. I truly thank Providence for saving you for me in this stage of my life, and I assure you without equivocation and /or mental reservation, that we will make these years together, the best of our lives.

Now, let us see if you will have me. I am 6' 1" tall, a slender 175 lbs.. People tell me I am distinguished looking, and rather handsome for my years, but I will let you be the judge, for it is all in the eyes of the beholder.

More important, my character and reputation are above reproach, and along that comes with it is wit and a sense of humor. I may add that I have an easy laughing personality, am articulate, solvent and rather successful within the purview of my goals and objectives in life, other than finding a soul mate, to share a boundless love with horizons unlimited.

I am an attorney by profession, and mostly retired, other than b eing on the Board of Directors of four different firms; two in New York and two in LaJolla, California. I travel to New York on a bi-weekly basis, and maintain an apartment there, as well as one in LaJolla. Yes, I am free with my time and will give my highest priorities share of love with a loved one. I enjoy the full scope of living, and especially when one is in love, for then the most simplest things become most eventful. I have a zest and zwal for living; have an affinity with nature --what with the beautiful Pacific; the spell-binding sunsets, the balmy, romantic nights with the scent of jasmine and orange blossoms in the air. I love music (opera, classical, Mantovani) the dance band music for our era, dancing cheek to cheek and just a heartbeat away (now do you see why I am simply delighted that you are 5' 7") scrabble, poetry, of which I write a little' and I want someone very special to share the depth and enrichment of all this, and more. It is worth striving for.

Moments of peace, serenity, tranquility, sweet repose and heavenly bliss. All of this is in the offering, if only with the right person. Happiness, contentment, adventure in living, exploring the explorable' the fulfillment of an infinite moment, ad infinitum.

Yes, I am an incurable romantic, most affectionate and have a tremendous amount of human warmth.

You have colored my life,Not in reds and yellows, That I understand; But in taupes and mauves And orange gold sunsets that defy INTERPRETATION.

Should this letter have any special meaning for you, and you can identify as a countepart when reading the same, and would like to have continued dialogue to last a lifetime' then please respond and send me more of your pictures, should you have anymore.

Yes, we should get together, and share a love that holds no equal, a lifetime of sweet and heavenly togetherness. In the meantime, look at the moon and the stars, they are the same for the both of us, and this we can share and dream of a love to which we both aspire.

Tenderly and Romantically submittedWilliam (CA.)

I shall be in LaJolla until the 13th of September, and my address is ......I shall be in New York from Sept. 13-20 and my address there is.....

9-20-87Dear Dottie ZimmermanTime flies quickly especialy when you are occupied with a lot of correspondence. To me it comes fast and sometimes piles up. Your letter was one of them. Don't know what list you have but it sounds like the COL mailing awhile back. COL incidentally failed over there months ago.

You state you have lived with your son for the last 8 years. Sounds like my situation 25 years ago when I took my mother under my rood. She was just 68. She was in poor health. a bundle of nerves and a very

8

determined woman. I kept her for 10 and a half years until her death 7 years ago. During that time she had four surgeries and a stroke which left her paralyzed for a period of time. She had a severe hearing loss. One of the surgeries left her blind. Later on she lost control of herself. I had to change sheets in the middle of the night and cleaning up the rug and floor. I spent most of my waking hours cleaning up after her. It's an ordeal I never want to go through again.

Even where I live now an adult apartment complex where the women outnumber the men by a toll of four to one. So many of them are nursing home candidates. It's rather depressing to me but since I no longer drive a car this location is good for me.

I am enclosing an introduction sheet which gives youa sketch of me.

It's interesting you mention Philadelphia. I lived there from 1942 to 1950. I I worked at Westinghouse Radio Station the station there KYW. For a while I lived at the YMCA on Arch Street and later on in Upper Darby. I've always felt at home in Philadelphia as I made many friends there but the ranks are thinning.

Right now in Ft. Wayne too the number I know are getting fewer in number. I thought COL was the answer. It didn't work. Since I have more letters to write I'll close for now.

Cordially,Lewis (IN.)

Here is the introduction sheet enclosed with the letterThe COL Corporation   We recommend this man highly and believe him to be honest, sincere, and personable. Because we vouch for him, we ask that you notify us at once if you are at all displeased with his actions or behavior. This is followed by a list giving details on his place of reside, physical attributes and other pertinent information about this man.

Dear Dottie, Zimmerman6-1-88How are you? It took me so long to get your address but I have it now. So will write you. I am just as lonely as hell. I wish you were here now. You are sure good looking at your age. I am 83 almost 84 in November will be. You are 75. Well I am ahead a little. See it don't make much age is on. It always the you feel. I have two dogs. They live in the house with me. Lot to be thankful for hope you like dogs. Do you have car? I got a car but the bitches in Topeka took driver licence away from me. I just bumped a car and knocked his tail light out of courfse when you get a little age on you. That

9

is why they took my driver licence I never had any wreck. In all the years I drove. I drove a car. What do you do now at 75? It is hell to get old but you cannot help it. I like to go fishing and hunt. I have the arthritis quite often stiff and sore for a few days. Then I am O.K. again. Well I wish we could make a djeal some way. So we could be together. I got three houses at this time and I got a pocket full of money . Don't do me much good can't spend it for anything I want. Only fishbait. I have been all around the U.S. and it the same there as here. This is a good place to live. Got two lakes here one is 4 miles from my door the other one 5 miles. I enjoy going fishing. I catch all I want I like to eat them also. Well what do you say, want to come l ive with me. I will pay all your expenses here no matter what it costs you just keep it all added up and I will pay you it all back when you get here. Bus would be best bet. Well you think it over and let me know I will be glad to hear from you. We will have a lot fun. As I said wish you were here and housekeeper. Wish don't mean a thing. Well let me hear from you please. You will have to come to Wichita Kansas to begin with. I will have someone to pick you up there and if you have a car you just drive it.

 Yours Truely,Fred (Kansas)

 Marion writes another letter
 Dear Dottie,Glad to hear from you. The picture was taken on Easter Day this year 1988. I do not believe you sent me your picture. I wish you would send me your picture now. I haven't had a suit on for so long I guess I still got one. I look all right. I am considered good looking. Always have been.
 You said something about buying a house down there. What is the price of a house down there. I got this small house here. It cost me $10,000 and that was six years ago. I want $20,000 for it now. But you cannot sell a thing here. I would want to sell this one before I bought another. Sorry to hear about your eye. O.K. I see you have a daughter and she has 3 children. How old is your daughter. She must ofr got married quite young to have a child 21 years old. Yes I like to fish. How about them storms they have down there. They seem to be bad.Well ab out all I can do is not plan on coming too soon. As it costs money to make a trip like that and I do have the money but I work hard for that money . So you been there for 10 years. Well you must like it there you have been there for some time. Just what do you think about these prices these days car

1000 dollars there is no car worth that much. I could get one but I won't pay that much for one. Well I have just about run out of something to write. You were a rather late write last time I got your letter yesterday. I begin to think I said something wrong in my letter to you and that you were not going to write to me anymore. Well hope to see you sometime but I do not know when right now. no the lady stays here is all mixed up. No worrie about her. She said she through with sex 20 years ago so I was through with her and all I got her here for is to make dinner and etc. I have told her to leave 30 times but she still stays I will get rid of her someday she is 76 years old. I guess if she dies that will end it. She has a brother that is a million dollar man but he is one big asshole like her. I never seen or heard of such people. They hate one another and that is it. Well I got to sign off.

Fred(Kansas)

and yet another letter from Fred

Hello Dottie, Glad to hear from you and hop this finds you well and enjoying life. Why I am rather unsettled. I can't come to Florida for this reason. I have two dogs and I can't drive my car. The dogs live in the house with me. They don't know what a cold winter is they are a lot cleaner than lot humans. It would take lot money to buy them for in fact they are not for sale. At any money they are my true friends. Why don't you come up here? I am 5'7" and one half tall. I guess you are taller than that. So you care too much for fishing I can't say I blame you too much. Weight 150 if you decide to come up here. I will pay your way. I do not have much of house for you to stay in but I guess we could make out some how. I have a mobile home right beside my house. It is quite nice I thinkso. I am sorry you can not drive a car. You see Dottie I was married one time and after 6 months she said she was off sex and moven in another bed so it was all over then. Now I lost my youth but I was younger at that time. It was no good for me but she told me of a few things that she had done it with someone else. O my birth date is Nov . 18 if it makes any difference. Well I do not believe in those signs. However I guess they are all right. Well you asked me what I did. I started out to be a farmer so I worked for reming arms. I was an inspector there. I bet you have a nice home yes or no? Well that is the reason I picked on you. I lost my youth and you are 75 years old. I guess you do not care much for sex anymore.

I never been to hav e it and I would care to go there. It would mean nothing to me. I been all over but that is one place I never been. A good rain here today it sujre was welcome we hadn't any rain for 5 weeks. Dottie what you got on your mind are you lonely? Have you got kids. I do not have any children. I wish some times I had some because I am getting old and t6hey might help me out but i have a cousin in eastern Kansas. He has two boys and 3 or 4 girls. He is worth a million dollars. He siad only time them boys come around him was when they want money. But he said they don't always get what they ask for. He does have a wife she is bitch in my words. I have never reached the million mark of this time but I got enough to get along on a pension of about $500 a monthy and the interest on my money comes in every month so I am getting along alright. O I have a head full of hair it is dark and gray. I chew tobacco smoke very little. I just puff it never inhale. about one or two a day. I do not drink just a couple tablespoonsfull a day that is about it and sometimes not that. Most of the time none. I will send you a picture of me but it's not the best but the best I can do at this time. O.K. glad you told me what kind of a car do you have. are you said you don't drive I wish you did. I have a nice little car runs like a new one but I can 't drive it as I told you they took my drivers licence them yourg hoars up there in Topeka thought I was too old. That is main reason they took it!!!!*****##### it's a shame we have p in the world like that. As I told you I had a housekeeper. She thinks she owns me I have told her 50 times to get out but she still stays she is mad all the time. I got to get rid of her some way.She will go to the phone and address herself a sMiss Lee. I told her to quit that.

    Fred (Kansas)

    A note from Fred of Kansas was enclosed it read "Hey I had a talk with the housekeeper here and she agreed to take care of my dogs if I wanted to go to Fl. so just how much of a deal would it be to get to your place. and what plane would I have to take could you give me some of the condition. Do you live house of your own or do you rent. Well I just might take a big idea to come down and see you?*************What do you think about it? Let me no in your next letter.

    since there were no more letters after this note I think we all know what Dottie thought!

8-13-87Dear Dottie:Thank you very much for your very nice letter and picture. I did not place any ad in "Friendly Singles". There must be some mistake. I once lived in Sarasota for 12 years and my wife died there 5 years ago. Presently, I'm not looking for a lady to correspond with - sorry. Thanking you again and wishing you all the luck in the world. I remain, Sincerely - Helmut (TX.)

Encl. picture

Here's a reply which came from a gentleman stationed at Howard C. Mcleod Correctional center

4-14-89Hello Dottie,Recently saw your name and address in a singles list. I felf I just had to commend you on looking so young, so lovely, and yes even so sexy for a 72 year old lady. Even though you look very young and lovely for your age I am far too young to seriously think about marriage to a woman of your age. However I would like to become your friend and who knows anything is possible.

Perhaps you will allow me to tell you a little about myself. I am 47 years old, weigh 150 pounds, hav e brown hair, and grey eyes. I don't drink and haven't in several years, also don't use drugs. I am an honest and sincere person. I haven been a widower for several years. Enjoy travel bosting, fishing, quiet evenings at home, and good food among numerous other things.

I feel it is perhaps only fair to tell you that I am currently serving time on a state prison farm because of a shooting incident in which I couldn't prove what actually happened. I have been in prison a few years and am hopefully looking forward to parole in the not too distant future.

Before coming to prison I ran a commercial roofing and sheet metal crew, and prior to that I spent eight years plus in the army in the 1960's.

Will close and anxiously await your reply.

Hopefully a new friendPaul (OK.)

10-22-87Dear Dottie,I am not inconsiderate - I appreciate you writing and sending your picture. You should know I am not looking for a woman as in -live in- or marry. I wrote to learn about other people, and their lives. Different areas have different thoughts and ideas. I soon learned that my thoughts and ideas were not the same. I quit writing. I can't travel and live in an area to learn about it. I didn't find what I was looking for so I dropped out. Why the people who write the lists continue to send out the names is beyond me. I haven't asked to be on a list for over two years. Thank you for being honest with me. I'll send your picture back to you - they cost money.Sincerely,

Bob (CA.)

7-10-88Dear Dottie Zimmerman my name is Mr. Donald ( ).

I received your name and address from a club for singles of men and women a few months ago, Portland Oregon , born and raised up in the Upper penninsula Northern part of Michigan. Integrity affectionate,realistic, and adventuresome person. I'm 5'7" tall, light blue eyes brown hair weight 160 lbs.. HSE white american good complexion nationality French Irish Scottish, prostestant religion, clean inside and outside. Don't use any kind of tobacco, liquor and never had any kind venereal disease or used a rubber on my_____.No drugs or dope. Borne 1912 Birthday August 5th. use to do alot of fishing in Michigan many b ig lakes , rivers water deep cold fresh in summertime. Trapping in winter months for small game animals, make my own snow shoes log cabins bows arrows bobsleigh toboggan skis. Birch bark canoe, crossbow gun, sling slingshots, pick wildcherries , pin cherries, chokecherries, fallcherries, black gooseberries, strawberrys,blueberries, cranberry delicious food, and fish. I like the spring, fall weather, everythingis all fantastic in it's beautiful colors.

May is time to pick mushrooms, in Ohio and part of Tuner. Three kinds of mushrooms in Ohio Black, yellow sponage and they are real rich delicious food. Ohio don't have every many natural lakes, most of them are man made lakes ponds.

I take a long walk in the morning sometime drive car out in the country roads.Beautiful in summertime, stop by a lake or river and watch the animals play together, birds, bees deer, think about you what kind person you are, tall or short, white or colored. Night time work on Ohio lottery numbers, 3 digit 4 digit 6 digit numbers, sometimes all night. I have won few dollars working on big one million dollar one.

Once in awhile take a drive to Cleveland, Ohio to fish or watch the sialboats motor about , or the boats fishing boats, row boats, and people in them city parks. My interesting things are rose garden flowers garden, bowling, fast horse races, oil paintings dog races people jet airplanes, eat ,

T.V., talking, long walks, vegetable gardens, play hors shoes, big blue skies, camping out, travel, children, amusement, sandy beaches, river lakes cameras, movies, western songs music.

Polka music songs, reading writing letters, bible western, short stories, cowboys cowgirls, ocean liners, entertainment, motel, hotel guitar, massage parlor, circus carnival, birds animals, antique cap guns, heaven radio,End Sincerely Donald(OH.)

12-28-91Hello - My Dear Friend Dottie,

I am Aramis - 35 yrs. old - 6'10" - 175 lbs. - 8 and a half "- Hazel - hairy chest - humorous - romantic - outgoing - affectionate - caring- creative - educated - adventurous - athletic - sensual - ambitious - uninhibited - loving - gentle -no smoke no drugs -social drunker - auto mechanic.

I like older women and I know you are alot older but my last lover was 65 yrs. old.

I like dining, dancing, concerts, movies, sex, parties, long walks, amusement parks, cars (old sports), kids, animals, photography, camping, picnics, swimming. Mellow music, slow dancing, classical, jazz, disco, opera, ballet. Love and enjoy seeing woman in sexy lacy skiimpy outfits like lowcut bras,garterbelts, G strings, black nylons, spiked heels, teddies, mini skirts, long evening stapless backless gowns.

Please send me your photo and if I'm not to your liking send mine back. (there is a full page picture pasted on the back of this letter. It is of a man and woman kissing passionately without clothes. It's caption reads "pure attraction"

Sincerely, Aramis (CA.)

Here is a reply to a letter Dot sent on 11-6-91

Dear Howard,

So nice of you to remember me. I may be interested in you but off hand I have no idea who you could be. Your name doesn't ring a bell. I have kept most of the letters that men have written to me and often go through them. I can't find yours. So what do you say we start all over again. Do you have a photo? I had my own personal ad published in Sheila Wood's column and I was surprised at the responce I received. But I am still looking for that down to earth person who is real. I know he is out there. Who knows maybe it is you. Could you fill me in on your background. Your likes and dislikes, what you are looking for in a woman. At least we have one thing in common. We both like Florida. My late husband's birthday is one day different than yours. His was the 23rd. of November yours the 22nd.. If you are anything like him you are O.K.. We do have a phone, but I prefer to write until we know each other better, anyhow I might be out if you call and then I would miss your call. I'll be looking forward to your reply. Do you remember I love perfume. If you still have my last letter the fragrance should linger on. Anyhow I'll spray this one. Hope you like the scent. Your friend Dottie

This man Howard never did answer Dot's letter so she just assumed that he was already taken.

6-20-91 Dear pretty lady:

I am a recent widower 74, 5'-10", 175 lbs, righthanded, allergic to housepets, have brown hair, brown eyes, keep tan year around and have lived in some parts of Florida since 1940.

I am a retired accountant traveled the states with the Engineering-Construction field and have lived in many of the 50 states. My wife was a widow when we married, her two children were grown with a family of their own. We were suited with each other, when I was ready to travel someplace, she was ready to travel too, or do anything else, I wanted to do and I miss it, too much.

She wrecked one of my cars while I was a way for a couple of days and if she had gotten over it I would never leave a car in her care again. But she never left the hospital. She was 15 years older than me and she would of been 90 now.

I have been an "Off & On-Photographer" since age 14 and have been driving since age 7. I have driven from Canada to Key West to Los Angeles and back several times and plan to do it again if I don't get a promising reply from you real soon.

I can also make you feel younger just by being around. I know everything that is good for you. I know how to keep us both healthy.

You are almost a petite size and have really taken care of yourself. So if you don't have any dependents or housepets or anything to hold you back then please drop me a long letter telling me all about yourself and end enclose a recent snapshot. I will do the same the day I hear from you.

If you don't have a snapshot and want to have one made I am

enclosing a certificate to hav e a free one made at Olan Mills Studios.

I am enclosing a sn apshot and if I were in Florida I would make you one.

I got rid of furniture, telephone and everythintg and had planned to leave the state before this but have been trying to find someone that would suit me and be compatible with.

William (TN.) I have lots of love to give

Quote:

"A secure and loving relationship gives you confidence and makes your immune system thrive."

Unqu ote.

Send my your birthdate and everything I need to know

If you are already suited return my snapshot and I will refund your postage. Thanks

footnote: on the back of this letter's envelope Dot wrote "not too good"

The outside information on this next letter was "lives in New York visits in August"

My Dear Lady 5 ft. 7" and Seventy nine

I thought I'd write to you and tell you a little bit about myself. I am your age but slightly shorter than you at 5' 6". I am neet and clean, non smoker I don't drink (underlined). But if by chance you'll have one then I'll have one. Have no ailments of any kind. I do not use drugs - not even the prescription type. Retired from the board of higher education from "Lehman's Herbert H. College" a New York City University. I am financially secure. Own my own home have no debts of any kind neither do I have children or grandchildren dependent on me. I love my grandchildren but seldom see them as they live in far away places like St. Petersburg, Fl., Staunton, Illinois, Sterling, Va., Dardanells, Ark...Huntsville Alabama. However once a year some of them will visit me in my home town. Lake Ronkonkoma which is located in Long Islands (New York).

To continue on I have lots to offer in a way of health benefits from the City of New York as a retiree from the New York city retirement system. So my little lady 5 foot six or seven I'd love to hear from you even though

Dottie Zimmerman

I have been corresponding with a lady in Jacksonville Fl. I made no commitments. But you seem to be the closest to my age and likes. "With God's help I shall be 79 on Oct 30" as I was born in 1912. On or about August 6th. I shall be visiting my grandaughter and her husband in St. Petersburg Fl. and from there on I could meet you face to face in a restaurant of your choice on a luncheon date or any place of convenience. In the meantime "Take my hand in Friendship" as I reach out to you with love. Stephen (N.Y.)

Dot responded to this Stephen of (N.Y.) and she responded honestly. This is what he then wrote her back.

Dear Dorothy,
Thank you for the nice friendship card and the quick reply. Here I am still admiring your photo as it radiates charm, and elegance. But living with son's and daughter's along with your grand children puzzels me and it does not encourage me at all. As for me I too have 5 grandchildren but all of them have their own home in Fl. , Ill., Virginia, Alabama. Only one lives with my father since his mother died. The poor boy just lost without her. At this writing I am not going to fill you in on my lifes history. But I can truthfully say that I would never live with any of my children or grandchildren for all the rice in China. I love them dearly but the umbilical cord was cut by their mother the minute they were born and the only help they got was from God and themselves. They made it on their own "Thank God". The sadest part in my life was when their mother passed away because I loved her so. That is why I thought of someone compatible with a meaningful relationship that has a home like I have so we can share each others house in the North and South as the season's change. It is the best way to go at my age - of course I have alot to offer for the one that comes my way and marries me as I have the highest respect for womanhood. So if I have a chance and with your permission I would like to visit with you if I possibly can.
With sincere best wishes and love to you and family Stepher (N.Y.)
p.s. I am enclosing a photo which I took yesterday on July 28 Sunday - I took it with a Poleroid Spectra self timer - So I didn't have to have someone snap it - like my son who is visiting his son in Illinois.

Oh this next batch of letters from this one gentleman is a gem.

Handwriting and spelling directly out of bizarro world. I'll do my best to interpret.

2-2-92   Dear Dottie

I'm not sure if my letter went to you. I found n envelope addressed to you and when I found the envelope I could not find the letter. So I don't know if my letter went or not. The ribbon is all gone on my typewriter it will be few days before I can get one as I have to order it. I phone in order I have your letter here a questions. So I'll answer in case my letter never gets to you. I have kids, some grand kids. Don't have drivers....but I sold my car but want to buy another. I have another. I have a handicap right now but when my foot heals I'll get around O.K.. I got a chance to make some easy money and will start within a week or two. I want to take a trip to Florida in the spring or summer maybe and I work long enough. I don't want to be rich but enough so I won't worry. My phone number is------------------ I've been so busy lately with junk mail I can't seem to keep up.But I'm throwing all away but some but it keeps coming. I did not even get some Valentine cards but you sent me one. It's 5 minutes to 6 in the morning I had my sleep and wake up a first 3 o'clock but I'll have to break out now. I'll write more love later Howard (WI)

next note is on a blank note type card . It is a cutsie woods scene showing two bunnies under a log   It is also from Howard.

Dear Dottie,

I think I wrote you about a page and a half then could not find it and lost your envelope your letter came in with your address on it.(can't decipher the next several lines but it is something about still having the address on some sheet of paper.)I'll answer your questions. I am a widower. I had 3 daughters all living and married and have children . I live in a one bedroom apartment.(more jibberish I can't decipher). I pay 149.00 a month including all except phone. Pay for it.It's big enough for 2 . I was born in July 16,1905 or 1925???? I'm cancer. Expert driver, 17 years of real estate 30,000 to 40,000 a year with an accident to me. Port Charlotte Florida 10 years Homossa Springs 2 years a trailor camp in central Florida. I like Florida all together 16 years in Florida. I will take you deep sea fishing if you marry me. I sold car today to pay off hospital but I'll buy one in the spring. I have a chance to make some easy money which I'll go for it. Can't go for my trip until my foot heals. Maybe May or June. How about a June wedding? Took hydra therma????? in school. I am better than some Dorothy under war in Hospital for my foot. (then there's something nurses and housekeepers and when he left they were doing it his way????)

next letter from Howard , Dot's little friend from some unknown parallell dimension goes something like this.......

Dear Dottie,
My typewriter is fresh out of ribbon so now you will see how poor my handwriting is.(I'd like to personally add that's an understatement) It will be a few days before I can get a few more. I'll call up one of the closest offices that handles the reel Smith Corona Electric ribbon. They have 2 in each package and each package I order 2 packs of word eraser. I must do alot of writing because I am out of ribbons more than I have them. I've been busy all day.(something about looking into a get rich scheme in Kansas and California) Now I don't want to be rich but I can use more than I have.(something about making thousands in a few days and being confused)(something about sending someone twenty five dollars for a deal) (Something about getting an answering machine at some shop for seventy five dollars or another one that is ninety four dollars) many paragraphs rattling on about making millions of dollars and feeding the starving children)(something about her picture being the best he's seen cause he's seen other pictures of women with their necks covered with big wrinkles)
Well it's 10:25 now and I just talked to you on the phone. I'm glad I called because that speeds up getting acquainted but I got to get to bed nowso I can get up at 7:30. (he goes on to explain how the nurses lift you out of bed)(then he tells her he doesn't like living in hospitals and nursing homes and if he can get a doctor or nurse to come along with him it's good)
Love and Kisses Howard

At last Howard sends a typewritten letter. I will type it exactly the way he did.

Dear Dottie: (starts out normal enough)

I HAVW A FEW MINNURWS SO ILL GET ON A FEW LINWS. I WOMDER WHY YOU DONT WTITE OR DID YOU GET MT LETTER AND DOD YOU WRITE. MAYBE ne of OUR LETT GOT LOST. IVE BEEN LOOKING FOR YPUR LEWTTER. ITS BREEN SNOEING LATELY. QUITE WATM JUST CORD ENOUGH TO SNOW BUR ITS SYPPOSED TO GET COLDER TONIGHT. I AM EWELL AS U CAN BE ANF HOPE TIY AEW THE SAME. HOWS THE WEATHER THERE. YHE LADT I NOTICED YR WAS ALMOST 80..RINDE I GOY SUPPER SO GET MY SUPPER

I STARTED THIS 48 HOURS AGO AND HA TO TALE OR OUT GOR A COUPLE BUSINESX LETTERS.OFF. DINT I NOW WHY YOU DONT WRURE. IM GETTKNG REASY TO MAKE A LOTT OF MONE UYULL GETTING AN ANSWSERING MACHINE ANF A CASSETTE RECORDER & player whaya been keeping you. i was CONFRATULATING MY SELD ON SETTING YOU TO WRUT WTIYE YO THEN AFYRT ONE LETTER I DONT SEEL TO HAVE TOY. YOU SAID I MIGHT BE THE SPECIAL ONE YOU LOOKING FOE SO I WAS TRYUNG TO BE REAL GOOD SO I CPULD BE THAT SPECIAL PARSON MY LAST WIFE DOWD ABOUT THREE YEATS AGO ANR I DONT WANT TO LIVE A;ONE THE REST OF MY LWFE.SO LIFE GOES ON ANF WE KEEP GETTING OLDER. YOU DONT HAVE TO WAOT UNTILL YOU GET A NEW UCTURE EOU JUST EWITR AND SEND THE PICTURE WEHN YOU GDT ONE. IM THJE DAME WZY. IVE GOY A COUPLE BUR THEU ARE NO GO OLD BUT I WANT TO WAOT TILL THE SNOW LEAVES AND THE GEADSS ID GREEN BEFOTE I TA KE MORE BUR IF YOU WILL EXCUSE A BAD PICTIRE ILL SEND YOU ONE AND UPU CAN SEND IT BACK WHEN I SEND YOU Z FOOD ONE. A B AD PUCTUTE ID BERRER THSAN NONE. BIT I WQUIRE MORE LETTERS. I WORRY TIIAY SOMETIIING MIGIIT IIAPPEN TO YOU MASY BE SICK./ WIYH YOU LUVINF WITH YOUR DAUFGTER I SOSE IT WOULD BE BETTER IF WE BIYGHT OUR OWN OT BUILD ONE. ANYWAY WE WOULD FIND A RETTY SPOY.O KNOW YOU ARE IN A PRETTY CITY BECAUSE I HAVE THROUGH SAE SOTA MANY TIMES BUT I NEVER SYOPPED. I LIVED ATPORT CHARLOTTE FO 1O YRARRS AND AT

HOMOASSS SPRINHGS FOT FOUR TEARS AND AT BUSNRLL FOR 2 YEATS. KHAKS IN THE CENTER PART OF THE STATR.

WELL I HAVE TO QUIT AND FALLING ADSEEP AR RGE SWITCH.

LOTA IF LOVE AND BE DURE TO WRIRE YOU OWE ME A LETTER NOW PAT ATTENTIOM TO MT ADDRESS SO YOU GET IT R LOYS A LOT OF LOVRE--KISSES

Howard (WI.)

1-10-91

Hello Dorothy,

Got your letter this morning.

Yes, I live in a home I paid for it.

I'm free to go and come as I please. I have a car and I like to fly. Would like to visit Fla. again. Sure hot here hope to hear from you again.

Sincerely, Jim (Washington, D.C.)

I believe Dot did not reply as the return address was the U.S. Soldiers Home.

I'm going to show you the ad Dot answered first and then the letter.

FLA. English-American male 71 5' 11", 165 lbs. on S.S., reasonable handsome, various interests. Seeks female for lasting relationship age, race not important

11-21-92 My Dear Dorothy,

I have just received your letter from the Globe. I thank you very much for answer.

I am divorced twice, but not ready to give up on finding someone to live in harmony with. I am not hard to get along with and am not looking for a lady with alot of money. I was born in Hull England, I came to the states in 1965. I have lived in Florida since 1977 except for 19 months in Arizona. I live in a log house I helped build on over an acre, quiet, secluded, but close to town. I love it! Maybe you would too. I have alot to talk about, which cannot be written, so Dorothy if you are interested in following up on this letter, please call me anytime or write and send a photo.

Yours sincerely, Leonard (FL.)

Here's another ad Dot answered . The ad went like this

FLA. Divorced, retired male early 60's, 6' 3", 290 lbs., nice home and car, easy to get along with. Seeks clean, intelligent, one-man woman. Age, nationality unimportant. Photo, phone

1-18-93   Hello Dear,
Thank you to answer my ad. I did not call you I was afraid I would scare you. I am a black man from Philadelphia. Divorced three years ago. I would love to talk to you . Hope to hear from you.
Sincerely, Linster (PA.)

I'd like to interject a small footnote here. I believe they talked but Dorothy was no way in hell moving back to Philadelphia. That is where she had lived most of her life and did not like the city. She felt blessed to be living in Florida.

no date   Dear friend,
I am answering you ad in the Globe. I am an honest man. I do not smoke or drink or use any kind of dope. I am in my 80's in very good health, have a very nice car and am anxious to meet a lovely lady like you. I am very please to get acquainted you. If you care for a photo I will send you one.   I will appreciate an answer from you. Thank you v ery much for an answer.
Bill (MD.)

You see at the same time Dot was answering singles ads she also ran an ad.

6-20-91   My Dear Lady:
How are you? Here's the reason for this letter. I was reading "Shiely Wood's Column" when your ad caught my eye. You sound very interesting and appealing.but most of all your sincerity. So I decided to write you this letter. I do hope you can understand my hand writing,but, please, allow me to introduce myself.
My name is Carlos. I am spanish descent my age is 55 years old. Single, and living alone in this city of wonders. I am dark, dark complextion, dark hair, built burly large weight 140 lbs. 5' 7" tall. Well first of all I am a retired war veteran with a passion for life. Besides my

social security I like to keep my mind occupied so I'm working at a private school as an instructor. This is my finest week and I do love what I am doing because am always around children and I do love all childrens and animals and nature of God. I hope that this short resume you'll have a idea who is writing this letter.

Dear Lady I will love to know you more, and begin an acquaintance . so will you answer this letter and at the same time went your fecently full length picture.......and your telephone number. I be glad to call you. I will send you a recently picture of myself. That is if you decide to answer this letter O.K. I will write you and tell you more about myself.

Well I quess this is all for now I am looking forward from hearing from you. Take good care of yourself, and may the Lord keep you in his arms always

Respectfully,   Carlos (OK.)

6-22-91

Dear Miss Florida,

Your ad really caught my eye, it was concise, well written and to thepoint - which is something I admire in a woman. Now a little about myself.

I hope you don't mind a younger man in your life. I'm 67 years old but I feel like 25. I'm always well groomed, no long hair, mustache or beard. I do not smoke or drink but do not mind if others do so, just as long as they can handle it properly. I'm 5' 7", 155 lbs.,black hair and blue eyes. Oh yes, I do not touch dope, that's a no, no period. I like to drive, swim occassionally and dine in nice restaurants but not necessarily in that order.

I have been here in Las Vegas about 4 years now. I have also lived in Sacramento, San Diego, Denver, Phoenix, Hot Springs ARK and New York City. Yes, I like to drive as you can well imagine.

I'm a mild mannered man, courteous, considerate, compassionate and affectionate with the right type of woman. I have never been locked up for anything and I'm in good health.

This picture was taken Nov. 1990, about 8 months ago. Hope it meets with your approval.

Hope this letter finds you in good health and spirits.

Pleasant dreams for now, Most Sincerely,   Joe (NV.)

6-21-91Hello Fla.,

Saw your ad in the Globe. Would like to get in touch with you.

I retired Air Force and live in U.S. Soldier's Home Wash D.C. I am 6 ft. tall weigh 190. No bad habits never tasted drugs don't drink. If you want to know more write.

Sincerely,Jim (D.C.)

11-16-89

Hi Dottie!

Got your nice letter and attractive picture in answer to my ad. Thank you very much. Since we live so close, I thought it appropriate that we know more about each other. Hopefully, you will agree.

I liv e alone in a nice home in Port Charlotte. Enjoy swimming (have a pool) most sports, a little traveling, home an social life. I have no children. I don't smoke and drink only very lightly. You must have known that good perfume drives my crazy. Hope to hear more from you.

Lovingly ,Carlton(FL.)

footnote, good perfume indeed but quite generic in brand.

Carlton take two

Dear Dottie,

Thank you for your nice letter telling me about yourself.

Hope you had a nice thanksgiving day with all the food. I hope your not spoiling that great figure. I must tell you the truth. I know you want that. Your letter indicates that you looking for a permanent relationship with someone, marriage etc.. This is probably the best way to go but it's really not for me, not yet anyway. Maybe I get carried away by your young look and girlish figure. I had ideas of your coming down to Port Charlotte, staying overnite (not a one night stand) but as a lover and friend. I still would like this but I'm afraid your ideas are different. I'm also concerned about your wants and desires. Don't you think it's good to clear the air before anything gets complicated?

I think you are a very good person and want you to have the best. So Dottie, you can tear this up and say "good riddance" or write and tell me what you think.

Still your friend,Carlton (FL.)

Dottie Zimmerman

10-5-91
Dear Dorothy,
I am enclosing the Photo you sent me. Your looks are super special but I am rather dissappointed in the way you missinterperted the letter I sent you. It had nothing to do with the love of your family or mine because "That's what life is all about Love" -love of family, friends, relationsw, but each in it's own way. The lady that I married after I lost my wife 14 years ago was a fine lady whom I adored. But when her grandson moved in with us all hell broke lose. He was Young restless dirty in his ways like all immature kids. Wanted to be spoiled by his grandma. as before and when I wanted to set him straight and fly right he threatened to kill me because I maried his grandma who gave him his every wish. His mother a divorcee likewise punched me while I was sitting in my car and screamed loud enough for the neighbors to hear. I alinated her mother's love.- (She hated her own brother who is a well to do Golf Co. Executive and owner of other enterprises mainly the Golf Co. named.................... I still maintain my good relationship with him and his wife. Needless to say that was my sad experience with family love. This lady i married had 3 homes a town house one on the beach one on the lagoon one where we supposidly wanted to make it our home and besides she had 10 other rentals where she derived her income. Nevertheless I was the one who supplied the means. It cost me $48,000 the short 2 years of happiness. But please don't misunderstand. I never gained or wanted anything out of our marriage but a home to stay in the winter and the summer to be spent in my own home in Long Island N.Y.. Was that too much to ask for? Just the same with all the interference from her spoiled brats I loved this lady and still do. But now she is in the clutches of her darling daughter who keeps her a prisoner in the home (her mother gave her) as a wedding present. There is much more but it would be too much for your ear to hear even in this letter with words. On Nov. 30 I will attend a wedding party of her grandson who is getting married. This grandson of my ex wife is the son of my ex wife also the owner of the golf co. by the name of............... So for the first time in 4 years I will be able to see her "I hope" without interference from her darling daughter. So in conjunction It was a blessing for me from God that I got away from her daughter's family's love. and I thank God for it. I came out alive and well. I glad that you did find a good man who is caring with a meaningful relationship but you can still be my pen pal . I always sign my letters with

26

Love because that's what life is all about.

Love , Stephen(NY.)

footnote, since Dot did live with her family she must have received a "trash the family" type correspondence from Stephen when he found out she lived with her family.   In light of that letter I'm almost sure she retaliated by telling him she'd found a man who loved her family.

6-27-91

Hi,

Your ad in the Globe on June 25th. attracted me. When I decided to scan the ads to see if I could meet someone I looked down the columns until I saw one from a woman 70 or older. And if the as wasn't from someone at least 70 I didn't bother reading it. Unlike most men my age I am not looking for someone younger. I am looking for a lady older than myself.

I am honest, caring and do not have any bad habits either. I do not drink or use drugs but I am still working. I am employed in the court system of New jersey.

I'm 5' 8", weigh 160 lbs., brown hair and blue eyes. I have no family committments and I am free to be wherever I choose. I am younger than you but that's the way I want a relationship to be. I am highly attracted to women older than myself. I am 57 and want to hear from you. It's hard to make an impression on someone in a first letter so why not write a letter to me with your telephone number or call me. I live at............................ If I'm not home leave a message on the answeringf machine.

Sincerely,John(NJ.)

7-25-91

Good day there,

My name Leonard. I am 80 years young. Do most of the yard work on one and three quarters acres. Am 6' tall. Do not smoke have a drink once in awhile. I have been married twice and been widower twice. Onetime after 47 years and the other time 12 yrs. so can't be all bad.

Hope to hear from you.

Leonard(FL.)

8-1-91

Hello, I have been planning to write this letter to you for quite awhile so here I go.

I'm a white male, 73 years old in good health. I weigh 190 lbs am 5'11" tall, slightly gray hair, blue eyes and well built for my age. I'm also a widower retired and have a good income.

I would like to sell my home and relocate to a warmer climate. I just hate these cold winters up here. I like outdoor activity such as fishing,swimming and yard work. I hope you will answer this letter and we can become friends. If you do please send a photo and phone number.

By for now Ken (NJ.)

Ken replied quickly after Dot's initial letter.
Sorry but I don't think it would work out.
Ken (NJ.)

6-22-91

Dear Madam,

Your ad in the Globe interests me very much.You sound so sincere and nice. I am looking for a lady of maturity in Florida, I like it there so much. I am 66 yrs. of age, a widower, no children, 5' 10", athletic n/s, n/d, am retired financially secure, Scottish by birth, Canadian by adoption. My wife was 78 when she passes away 2 years ago. I am looking for an older lady, it's a little difficult. I'm very affectionate, loyal, honest, very clean, cultured, love the outdoors, home life, gardening, travel, walking, reading.

I am looking forf a permanent and loving relationship with the right lady and I feel that you are the one for me. I have so much to tell you of my life but I shall wait until my next letter. I hope to have the pleasure of hearing from you soon. I shall be counting the days. Hope you like the photo, taken last year.

au revoir, Very Sincerely,John (Canada)

8-12-91

Dearest Dorothy,

Your letter and photo were so very delightful, and your perfume fills my livingroom, you are so seductive. I am so attracted to you. You must be quite a houseful with all yourf family liv ing together. I hope that we can all meet one day, do you think that you could leave all of them to live

28

with a man. I'm very healthy, active, love to travel like to go back to my homeland for visits, Scotland is so beautiful, lotss of my friends there, but it's windy and cool.

Vancouver is a beautiful city, but now Canada is very expensive, we have to pay for our wonderful social and medical system. My only relative (my sister) lives in Toranto, I go there fairly often for a v isit, she is married with 2 married daughters and grand children. I am very frustrated but I don't play around. I am waiting for the right lady to love. I have my ideals, sex without love is of no consequence, and I believe that one day I shall meet my sweet love and then all my passion and tenderness I will give to her.

When I go to sleep I hope that I shall dream of you. I have your photo by my bedside, the perfume still lingers to excite me in my room. Take care and God Bless.

Much love,John (Canada)

12-17-92

My Dear Dorothy,

I am deeply sorry for being so late in getting in touch with you. Firstly I had to go North for an emergency, one of my daughters. Secondly I have had such a overwhelming reply to my ad, that I haven't been able to keep up with the mail. So I wish you all the very best.

Sincerely,   Love, Lawrence (FL.)

8-7-91

(I'll use both sides of this paper because I'm so longwinded)

You sounded just scrumptious. I loved, the 5'7" and pretty. Also your age. I'm very interested in meeting an older woman too. You're not a bit too old for me and I mean that sincerely! I am super relocatable. All my life I've wanted to try Florida and haven't even visited there ever. I'v e traveled alot lo)*Besides - your ad says "Age unimportant" and I'm holding you to that.Dear Miss #7080L What an awful name! We'll have to change that. I can't imagine why I've waited so long to write to you. I wanted to right after seeing your ad but I'm the world's greatest procrastinator for sure. Wish I had a photo to send you. I'm about 6' tall cheating just a tgad w/ cowboy boots. Have light brown hair still hav e two thirds of it. and a mustache, and I'm proud to day still weight only

150# w/ no beer belly, which is quite a feat in Milwaukee! My jeans size is 32"w x 35" l. So you can imagine I'm still fairly trim and slim. You are too from the sound of it. Surely hope you're still foot loose and fancy free Sell you on our meeting. My interests board games like chess, cards, backgammon, trivial pursuit, monopoly, mille bornes, scruples, rummi-kubes, etc. etc.. Music of all kinds, but especially bluegrass, big bands, swing dixieland, old-time (waltz, polka, schotti sche etc. dancing, some sports but I'm not a sports fanatic, traveling, home life, walks, fireplaces, swimming, tanning, and just spending endless w/my special one and only! I'm a one woman man let me assure you no womanizer here. No wimp either. I like to wear the pants and I hope you're an old-fashioned girl.

I have an incredible sense of humor am a c ollege grad and have all kinds of handyman skills interests including electrical , painting, plumbing, home repair, housekeeping, auto repair, yardwork, gardening, etc. etc,! Even do windows. Being an old kraut (German-American) and I'm not afraid to pitch in. The only thing I can't do is wash dishes because I have very dry hand skin and cannot use detergent at all nor bleach. I'm also a lousy cook, but hey, you hav e to have something to do , eh?

Dear please write or better still give me a call. You'll be glad might even be meeting each other before August is out. I'm only going to be here at a friend's for a few more days. her son is here too so please call person to person and talk only to me. If you are strapped financially I can cut it short, and call you back on my m.c.i. credit card. I'n not in good financial shape at present but that will change when I just meet the right someone. I've been semi-retired for 3-4 years but I'm in top health and w/20+ years of auto food service and personnel mgmt. experience should have no problem in Florida, getting a part-time at least, job. I'd like to work 20/30 hrs. a week, and they say it's best for a relationship, anyway not to spend all day everyday looking at each other getting in each other's hair etc. did you find that to be true when married?

I haven't been to a doctor for about 4 years and then it was only to a dermatotogist for my hands (the dry skin mentioned earlier) Use a cortizone salve to control it, but 1 tube lasts for months. Other than that I have no drugs in my life whatsoever nor have I ever! Do drink beer but only beer and I do not smoke at all except for an occassional cigar.(outside the house if you wish).

I'm very considerate, kind and gentle , although very domin ant. I'm also con sidered attractive I guess though I'll let you be the judge. Run your long legs (??) to that phone and / or get a letle w /a sexy picture of you in it to me as soon as you lay my letter down!!! That's an order.

Love, Tom(Wis.)p.s. Great Ad!

footnote , his return address was the EDGE-O-TOWN MOTEL

Just to break things up here I'll show two ads for men which Dot had clipped out and saved:

WISC. Nice gentleman, 73, retired a long time, homes in Fla. and Wisc., has best of everything. Seeks honest, attractive, slim lady, 50 -60. Recent photo please.

FLA. Chinese male, 80, looks great for his age, slim and handsome. Seeks lady, 65-90, for marriage. Serious only. Race unimportant.

12-19-91   Here was a Christmas card from one of the men Dot was in correspondence with.

Dear Dorothy to you and all your loved ones. Wishing you every happiness at this Christman season and throughout the new year.   Frank

6-22-91

Read yor as and decided to pean a few lines. I'm a single white male 66yrs, of age 5' 10" tall 162 lbs. and in pretty good shape so far. Clean and neat don't drink or use dope. I'm semi retired (you may not like that) as most of my life is spent working. I think a man should work if he is alive. I work in home improvement like construction . Would like someone to have and relax with. A good woman and you seem to be the perfect lady to spend the future with. I'm not a night person either and I'm not the type to go with just anyone. Too many things like aids going around and I just don't need that. Life is short enough as it is. I'm sure you feel the same way. Would like to get to know you as you sem to be a very gracious lady and caring. Believe you would be a lady a man can be proud of and nice to relax with. A good loving woman is hard to find and I will never marry a woman my age . If you wish I could get a photo for you. I receive S.S. and have my VA. pension from the Marines. Was in World War 2. Am not handicapped in any way but was scarred a few times. There is no problems though. Served in China after the war as well. I have other letters to recognize so I guess I'd better close for now. If you do write or call and have questions fell free to write back.

RespectifullyLes (Indiana)

On this envelope Dot wrote that she answered the ad but noted that he was too far away.

This next letter was a reply that was undated.

Dear Globette,

It took me awhile to come up with that salutation. I wanted something catchy to show you I have a sense of humor.

four years ago I moved to Florida form New York. so far I haven't met anyone. Many ye3ars ago, I answered an ad such as yours and was successful in meeting someone. Now I'm hoping success will repeat itself.

Let me now give you a run down on myself. I'm retired collect a pension and social security. I'm white 5' 8", 170 lbs. and am 63 years old. My idea of a pleasant evening is a fin e dinner followed by a good live show.

If this letter interests you, you may write to me at the above address.

SincerelyGeorge (FL.)

6-21-91

Dear Lady,

A great as I must say, I shall come to the point, I also live in Florida West Palm Beach, I am 125 lbs. in weight with no bad habits, and very easy to get on with. I am English from jolly old london, and have lived here 19 years, actually we came here for my wife's health. And she passed away 3 and a half years ago. It was a very wonderful marriage believe me, I do not intend to get married again and I hope you are of the same way of thinking, we could be a confort to each other and I do enjoy kissing and cuddling, and anything else if you wish. May I suggest you telephone me as soon as possible, you will enjoy talking to me I am sure. But please do not delay, i shall look forward to your phone call.God bless you dear lady,

I am looking forfward to your call

yours truly,Morris (FL.)

8-12-91

Dear 7080L,

I see your ad in the Globe and thought I'd answer it. I am 76 years old was married 50 years plus 6 months when my wife passed away 5 yrs. ago. I lived in Jacksonville, Florida for 13 years until my wife got sick and came back to Mass. I sure would love to meet you. I know we could make a go of it, Ask me any questions and I'll answer them truthfully. Hope to hear from you soon. I live with my daughter here so if you care call me at.............My address is...........

Henry, (Mass.)

6-23-91

My dear pretty lady,

I am interested in you because you live in Florida. I also live in Florida hav e a mobil home, it's getting to be a little expensive for me lately because of a high lot rent, electric, telephone bills, gas bills, taxes etc. you know how it is. I am on social security and a small pension and it's tough to get along these days. I would like to find a partner that will share expenses with me or I am very anxious to sell the mobil home and go with someone who would share expenses. I am 73 years old, handsome in good shape 5' 9 and a half", 185 lbs.

I am a World War 2 vet decorated and belong to the American Legion am a life member. I was a construction worker and labor boss in New York City for 30 years. I live in Florida 20 years and have no dependents. Would like to find a woman with no dependents so we c an be free to do whatever we like. If interested call me at............I am a white male a man's man. I did everything in my day and I hope I can fill the bill for you. Long John . If you would like me to call you send me a photo if you have one and your telephone number. I will call you .

Thank you

P.S. I am a very loving and caring personJohn (FL.)

footnote : on the envelope of this letter Dot wrote "Share expenses, No"

7-14-91

Dear Dorothy,

thank you for the very nice letter. You too sound like a very nice lady.

33

All of my family (children are grown up). I am living with my daughter. I am retired. I sold my house that I live in. It was in Fla. I do not have any bad habits. I don't smoke, I don't drink (only water) I do not use any kind of dope. I am in very good health. I have a very nice car. I lived in Fla. for about 8 yrs. I live in Deerfield Beach. I will tell you alot more when we meet. You can depend on me, that I am a honest trueful man. Yes I would relocate in Fla., because I love Fla. The picture I am sending you was taken in 1990. I am coming to Fla. in a few months. So write me a nice sweet letter and tell me more about yourself. I do alot of Gospel singing. If you want I will send you one of my tapes. Don't forget to send me a very sweet letter and a picture of yourself.

Thank you for a sweet answer

May God bless you I think you are a very sweet lady

Bill(MD.)

There was no date on this next letter.

Dear Pretty Lady,

I would like to get in touch with you and become your friend. I am getting tired of the cold winters in Buffalo and I thin k we could be in for a bad one this year. They say when you get a hot summer you can look forward to a cold winter. Well enough for that I have a sister who lives in Datona that's near Fort Lauderdale but I don't like to go to see her because she is always loaded with her family and friends so I just take a rain check when she invites me which is very often. Well I won't go into my life in Europe that is Scotland but we will later. I am a citizen of this country a good many years but I am retired. I was a brick mason and also a security guard but I am taking it easy now . I hope to hear from you soon. Your very good friend.

p.s. Please write

Johnie (NY.)

12-17-91

Hello Dorothy,

I did not write much because I do not write very good anymore. I do not drive because I am blind in the right eye. I have my daughter living with me and she takes me where I want to go. My daughter works long hours and I get awful lonesome here. I have 3 boys and 1 girl by my 1st.

wife and 3 step daughters by my 2nd. wife. All are very good to me. I came to Florida in 1945 lived in Ft. Lauderdale until 1974 then moved to Ft. Myers and moved to Plant city in 1990 because my wife had 3 daughters here. I was a mechanic al contractor before I retired. The picture I sent you was taken just before I sent it but it did not come out very good. This picture was taken about 2 years ago. If you are interested in me please call me collect. I can talk better than I can write.

waiting to hear from youLeonard (FL.)

This next letter is yet another dateless...get it dateless????? letter

Hello there,

My name is Bob 6' tall 200 lbs. brown eyes younger than you but I am sure you can handle it. and satisfy me. Yes I would lov e to live in Fla. IU am free, and could move anytime. Write and I will come down to meet and make nice plans. Write pretty one and I will come to you.

Very Sincere,

Bob (PA.)

7-5-91

Dear Ms.

My name is Paul I'm 41 years old, 5' 9", 185 lbs. with black hair and moustache. I'm a semi-retired self-employed electrician and part time school bus driver. I have an 18 year old son named Bob and we live in a 2 bedroom house in Mass. I have several interests such as music, good movies, beach walking and yard sales. I like rythmn and blues and play the bass.

In recent years I've been thinking of relocating to Florida and working part time. Well I'll be brief for now. Please write back if you'd like to correspond.

Sincerely

Paul   (MA.)

10-12-89

My new sweet friend dottie:xxxxxxx

Thanks you very much for your very nice and sweet letter of Sept 21 answering my ad in the Examiner. Wishing you are feeling fine.

Up to now I received 165 letters from my ad in the Examiner but your letter is different, that is why I am answering it now. By your letter reads that you are a very sweet, lovely, affectionate, lovelingly, very warm etc. woman. By your letter I am sure you have a lot of love to give so lets be good and close friends because it seems to me you are the woman I am looking for, you sound like a dream. Your letter is very short but tells me alot about the kind of woman you are and you are the kind of woman I need and I am looking for. So try to answer all my questions, so we can become bery close friends and don't waste too much time. Don't you think so, sweet Dottie? You wrote "I would lov e to meet and get acquainted." I do want to meet you too so, lets first write some letters so we know more about each other, what we are looking for, what we want etc. etc, and then we can talk about meeting. Don't you think so?

You wrote your birthdate is May 9, 1912, so you are 77 years old. I was born May 20, 1918 so I am a Taurus too. I am sure you know what Taurusw means. There is alot of passion, affection. love, etc. between us. I don't believe in Astrology but sometimes read about it. Taurus people have a very good heart but like the bull once their mind is made they are very hard to change. They are great lovers and very warm and live very close to his woman etc.

Have you children. Do you live alone? Do you own home? Are you looking for a pen pal or something closer? How long have you been living alone? Are you lonesome? Are you really looking for company or just a pen pal to pass time? I received a lot of letters but there are too many ladies who are looking forf a penpal and other are just playing games to pass the time to entertain themselves.

In your next letter I will appreciate if you send me your picture. Most of the ladies says as you did I have no picture, have some made etc. Yes, I like perfume too and use men's cologne in my body and hankies. I like to keep myself very clean and like a woman who is clean too. I take bath daily and change my clothes. I love a clean woman.

As I told you in my ad I live alone, I have no children or dependents. My wife 3 years ago died from Alzheimers and Diatetis I took care of her at home as I did not like to put her in a nursing home. First I thought to live alone but after two years I found it is very hard to liv e alone so I started looking for company, but it is hard to find the right person. There are too many ladies looking for something sometimes they don't know what they are looking for but up to now I am living alone. Ladies over 60 want to get married too fast and I don't care to get married till I know or we know each other very will. Old people marry too fast and divorce too fast too. 80% of the marriages over 60 don't last 6 months. Now I am living alone, I don't like it but I am living in peace and when I have company then I will want to continue living in peace too. I own a very good brick home with central heat and air.all paid a long time ago. I don't drink, smoke or gamble, I am a very clean mind in body and mind but I need company as I am very much affectionate, warm and have alot of love to give. I think I can give you a very good company as I have alot of love to give you and make you very happy. I am sure you are very lonesome specially at nights and you need a lot of love and decent, honest clean company. Don't you think so Dottie?

If you sincerelyh and honestlyh are looking for love and good company I am sure I can give you what you need so much. I can make you start living a different life the one you need and want so much.

You wrote "I am a warm lov ing person looking for the same in return" if that is what you are looking for them we must talk and try to be good and close friends and try and meet in the very near future perhaps in 6 weeks. Don't you think so honey?

To close I do thank you for answering my ad and I will be waiting for your answer. I think I have what you are looking for and plenty of it for you.

With Love (underlined)

xxxxxyour new friend,Ramon (FLA.)

My phone is....... I will be waiting for your long letter and photo.

Do you like long letters? I think you are very romantic You sound very, very sweet and lovely I should like to have all your love

11-12-90

Dear Dottie,

Thank you so much for your nice letter, came a little late though. I'm currently seeing someone. Much luck in your search.

Sincerely,   TL1noo34M (FL.0

7-18-90

Thank you for your reply Dottie. I wish you good luck too.

with friendship,John (FL.)

12-30-89

Dear Dottie,

I hope you had a very merry christmas and will have a happy new year filled with peace, joy, happiness, good health, and much prosperity.

I selected your name and address from a list of names and addresses sent by FINDERS KEEPERS CLUB, Evensdale, Iowa. Even though you live in Sarasota, Florida, and I live here in Dayton, Ohio, I could see no harm writing this letter. As the Bell System has said, "Reach out and touch someone." And, that's what I'm trying to do!

The following is a copy of your as as it appears in the above issue: Age 77, 5' 7" 120 lbs. Dottie I. Zimmerman, (address). Widowed, gray blonde hair, dark eyes, high school, I'm a grandmother. Don't drike. Likes collecting coins and antiques, movies, scenic drives, travel. Is caring, clean, loving, open minded. Seeks tall 70 yr. old or older who is financially secure."

I'll briefly tell you a little about myself. First, I must warn you, what I'll tell you will not make the best seller's list. (smiles). As you c an see, my name is Howard, my age is 57, (my date of birth is the 22nd of March 1932. I stand 5' 5" tall, and my weight is 165 lbs. I'm single, have no dependents, have never been married. I don't smoke, drink, nor do I use drugs. On the other hand, I'm not annoyed by those who smoke and/or drink in moderation. Live and let live, I always say.

I'm an easy going black fellow, who is serious with a great sense of humor, I'm open-minded, honest, and love to give and receive TLC. I love to laugh and make others laugh, as well. I'm sensitive to other's needs. Some say, I'm too sensitive, I tend to agree. I like animals especially dogs and cats.

I know I don't fit the bill of the man you are seeking. My age is wrong, I'm too short, and I'm a black man. My main reason for writing this letter is to pay you a compliment. With all respect to you, a lady, I find you to be a very attractive, and beautiful young lady. It seems like you have a very lovely figure. There's no doubt in my mind, but I'm very certain you have been told that many times, and will be told many times in the future.

I'm certain that you have received many letters, and will receive many more. While you have the difficult task of choosing Mr. Right, perhaps you'd enjoy exchanging letters with me. Once you get to know me, you'll see I'm a very nice fellow. I only bit if you will not answer my letter.

(smiles)

Now more about yours truly. I don't like to argue or fight, however, if I must argue, then let it be in a systematic manner. I believe in Women's Lib, that is equal pay for equal work. I still enjoy treating a lady like a lady with respect, kindness, warmth, and consideration.

I hope you aren't thinking, I'm trying to c onvince you that I'm an angel, because I'm not .I'm just a man who is trying to live his life by high standards. I do try to live by my "GOLDEN RULE', which states the following" 'I WILL TRY TO TREAT YOU IN THE MANNER THAT I WANT YOU TO TREAT ME, OR I WILL TRY TO TREAT YOU IN THE MANNER YOU DESIRE TO BE TREATED." Some times it isn't easy. In these 57 years, I have learned that all people do not wish to be treated as I wish to be. There are times, however, when I do become just a little naughty!(smiles)

I enjoy swimming, movies, walking in the woods, long drives in the country, walking in the rain and the snow, driving in the rain especially at night, and I enjoy driving in the snow at night. Also, I enjoy sensets and sunrises, moon lit nights, lightning and thunder, the country side during the wintedr when it is covered with about a foot of snow that has not been disturbed, and un der a clear blue winter sky, and I enjoy photography. Also, I enjoy quiet evenings at home reading, watching tv, listening to easy listening music, music from the big band era, jazz, dixieland jazz, classical music, and country and western music.

Since I work the 4 to 12 shift, I enjoy only two quiet evenings at home a week. I am a public servant, employed by our Federal Government, and work in data processing. St present, my off days are Saturdays and Sundays, but my off days are subject to change. Our shop's working hours are similar to those in hospitals, 24 hours a day, and 7 days a week. We never close.

If you are ever up past the mid-night hour, if you would like to talk by telephone, please feel free to call, and I'll pay for the call. I' usually home from work by 12:45 a.m. , but sometimes later. My telephone number is................ Would be very delighted to talk with you. If on the other hand, I had your tlelphone number, and knew the best time to call, then I'd call you.

If you have any questions you want answered, please feel free and ask. I shall answer any and all questions as honestly as I can. I like to place my cards on the table, face up.

I'm looking forward to hearing from you very soon ! Until then, I hope all your news will be very good news.

Sincerely yours,   Howard (OH.)

7-15-90

Dear Dottie,

I truly hope this letter doesn't impose upon you, but I was given your name, address & a small cut out picture of you by a guy, who said he got it from a pen pal listing. All I know is : Lady, you ar indeed one beautiful woman! Which brings me to the focal point of my letter to you, and the current situation I'm presently faced with.

Dottie I am at present incarcerated. I have no family, no friends, no contact with anyone on the outside world and I am desperately lonely! If you have ever remotely felt complete abandonment, then I'm sure you can understand how I'm feeling. Is there a chance even a slim one that we could establish a correspondence and perhaps become friends? I'd be forever grateful to you. If I have offended you by writing , please accept my apologies.

Have a fantastic day!! Sincerely yours,   Delman (OH.)

12-23-89

Dean Dottie,

I was just looking through a notice from letters of friendship club, and glanced thru the section with "older" woman. Your photo caught my eye immediately! Even compared to the other sections of younger women. Your figure stands out! and I love your legs!!

Before I go any further I'm 37 years old. Does that bother you? How old are you? 50-52 maybe? I enjoy movies, music, sports, dining out and reading. I'm 5' 9" tall and weight a fit 175 lbs. . I do not smoke, drink, nor use drugs.

Yours,Ken (Pa.)

1-30-90

Dear Dottie,

Your ad and picture in finders keepers attracted my attention and prompts this reply. From reading your ad I believe we share some common interests.

I'm divorced 7 yrs., caucasian, 6' 2" x 180 lbs. Like you I am caring, clean, loving, well educated, diesease free and very open minded. I'm 67, very active and relatively healthy. While I'm certainly not wealthy I am financially secure. I feel too, that I'm emotionally secure and certainly secure with my sensitivity and sexuality. In dating I find that many women are quite insecure with themselves. For that reason I much prefer older ladies who are more apt to be secure with themselves, their emotions, sensuality/sexuality, etc. Ladies who can accept themselves and are not out to prove something to the world. From what I could tell from your picture -- it was too clear --you are a very, very attractive lady. I believe it was taken while you were wearing lingerie. Do you pose that way often? Hopefully so, so you can send me a picture of two as I do love lingerie and figure photos.

I plan to be in the Tampa/St. Pete areas early in March. If our correspondence , and perhaps a telephone call or two, works out maybe we will arrange to meet each other at that time. That is, of course, if you are interested.

Sure would appreciate receiving a picture or two and your telephone number so I can call you.

Looking forward to hearing from you soon.

Sincerely,Ira (CO.)

More from Ira

Dear Dottie,

I apologize for not answering sooner. I've had the flu and just have not been able to shake it. So I've not had the energy to do very much.

Then last week a firend of mine was killed in an auto accident so it was rather unsettling as it was quite a shock. Otherwise, things have been pretty quiet around here. We've had some rather chilly weather but no rain. We need the rain badly or we will pay for it next summer in the way of drought as this will be the third dry year in a row.

Have you had any more replies to your ad? I've thought about running an ad in the globe or Examiner but haven't done so. Don't know quite what to expect. When I talked about pictures I thought I might have one or two that would be suitable but haven't found one yet. Then I thought about taking one of myself with a polaroid camera but haven't felt like it, but by the time I hear from you again I'll have one to send you.

I try to be honest. We talked about your picture...The way you are wearing lingerie.... well I like pictures like that or other revealing photos and would appreciate anything you send along those lines. I know you said you were modest but I suspect you have had some experiences before the camera and may even have some photos laying around. Send what you can.

Along that line, inasmuch as I'm going to have to have some taken is there anything inparticular you would like to receive. I may have to find someone to take them b ut mayby I can arrange that.

So far I haven't fixed up anything about going to Florida but it still looks like April. Hopefully, we will be able to spend a day or two together so that we can become better acquainted. Sounds like fun doesn't it?

When you wrote you said you would write a longer letter next time. So I'll be looking forward to receiving your letter. Hope to hear from you soon.

Always,Ira (CO.)

again! again! Ira
Dear Dottie,
I received your letter with the pictures and the Valentine card. Thank you very much.

It seems as though the postal service is deterroriating. For some reason it takes from 6 -8 days to get a letter from you. About 6 -8 days after the postmark I receive the letter.

Dottie, I have been doing some rather serious thinking. There is an awful lot of real estate between us. I'm certain that if we were to meet and spend a day or two together we would have a wonderful day or two together. But what if we wanted more. Because of distance there'd probably be nothing but infrequent visits and that I'm sure would lead to considerable frustration on both our parts, and I don't think we need that.

So, I think we better cool it for awhile and reassess where our heads are. I'm going to send your picture back even though they are very provocative and interesting. When I get to Florida I'll give you a call and we'll see where we go from there.

Sincerely,Ira. (CO.)
end of the Ira transmission !!

1-25-89

Dear Dottie,

My name is Joe. I received your phot, address from Friendly Singles. You looked so pretty the way you were dressed and posing for the camera! I loved your snale necklace and large cuff bracelet and sexy neglige (or perhaps that's a bathing suit?) I just couldn't resist writing to you.!!!

Chronologically I'm younger than you, but I've always preferred older much more mature and sophisticated ladies as yourself. I didn't send a photo on purpose but I am considered handsome. I will send one if you request it.

Let me tell you ab out myself. I own manage a large video rental business. I am also vice president of the Chanber of Commerce. I'm president of a fine arts and crafts gallery. I'm a jewelry designer, also design custom designed sweat shirts for ladies (no two alike). I'm also a professional musician/singer/songwriter with a C & W dance band. I play several instruments. (Nashville affiliated). I write love songs (C & W and Easy Listening). Do my own recording As a jewelry designer I create unusual and large pices of silver and turquoise jewelry!!! *I'm enclosing a silver and turquoise matching filigree cuff bracelet and ring that I think would look great on you. Please accept my gift in friendliness. I promise there are no strings attached.

It would please me so much if you would correspond w/me & perhaps call me "collect of course". My phone number is.............. I have a large home with secluded swimming pool and patio. I'm financially secure. Own much property here and in TX.. I would love to spoil and pamper you with TLC & the best of everything.

I'm tender generous kind and extremely affectionate and loving, a true gentleman. I don't drink but love to dance! (have won awards for waltzing) I'm a hopeless romantic still searching for the old happy ending. (where man and woman meet, fall in love and live happile ever after). It can be that way if two people are willing to work at it. I know I am. I just never met a lady who was willing to try that hard.

If you want to know why I prefer older women I'll try to explain: I find the sophistication and maturedness of an older woman to be very emotionally stimulating. I also find an older ladies skin sometimes with wrinkles (I call them character lines) I find them to be very sensuous. I would love to hold your hands and kiss them, and hold you tenderly in my arms and I'd be proud to be with you anywhere in any crowd. I find you very beautiful and simply gorgeous!!!!!!!!!!

If you're wondering about my age well, I'm no kid (at this point he drew a smiley face) I've had 12 yrs of college (BFA degree and two trade degrees) I'm a vet of the U.S.A.F. and I'm a very unique individual!!!!! Age is a matter of the mind - if you don't mind it doesn't matter!!!!!! I don't necessarily search for older women but they seem to be attracted to me, as much as I'm attracted to them!!!I can't quit staring at your photo. You mystify me . Were you or are you a movie actress? If you decide that there's no future for us together would you still be my very close friend? and would you let me send you jewelry and would you please me by wearing it?

I'm old fashioned. I like courtship. I believe men should be gentlemen and women should be ladies (as it was in the 40's and 50's).I'm not into the games that people play with each other's hearts these days. I believe a man's lady should be his queen and she should be treated with great gentleness and tenderness and she should be given the courteousy and respect she so justly deserves. I derive my happiness from making other people happy!!!!! Would you allow me the honor of making you happy? I'm your knight in shining armor waiting on his trusted steed to take you to his castle to make you my queen!!! footnote time , yes right smack dab in the middle of Sir Lancelot's speech. On the next page of this letter he has drawn a castle a knight on a horse and he has labeled the knight "Sir Knight Joe" . The castle has the words "your castle" written above the tower. They are written in a circle with an arrow pointing to the castle. At the bottom of this masterpiece is written. "I'm better at painting or drawing land, snow and seascapes). Which is very insightful as if you saw this picture without an explanation you'd have the urge to grab a magnet and attach it to the fridge. nuff said now back to the letter. Will you be my valentine? (he drew a heart) *Please write me or call!!!!!!! I'll be CRUSHED if you ignore me!!!!!!God bless you and keep you safe!!!!

Sincerely, Respectfully and very affectionately,Joe (N.M.)

Don Quixote continues.

2-2-89   Dearest Dottie,

You liked my first package so much. I hope you'll enjoy these trinkets just as much.

I dreamed about you last night. I dreamed that you came to visit and we went for a candle lit dinner and then went dancing in the moonlight.

Then we sat down under the stars, held hands, and shared each other's dreams of true happiness!!! I kissed your hands (one at a time) looked in your soft, loving eyes, kissed your sweet lips, then you put your head on my shoulder and you touched my face with your soft hand and told me you really cared, then we drifted off to sleep arm and arm.

Dottie would you tell me your waiste size please. I want to make you an Indian designed concho belt.. Also do you have pierced ears?

Hope you got my last letter and hope you still like me after finding out my age. Hope my photo didn't displease you. To me you are a real queen and I'll always treat you so, with the respect and dignity you so deserve!!!!! I'm making you a squash blossom necklace befitting a queen!!! I'm also making you a tape of my best songs. I had a hard day today. Moving, (next to the word moving is a frowny face followed by the word Ha!, where does he get his material?) I'm moving to my new house with an inground pool and patio. Do you swim? I love it. Great exercise. My mailing address and telephone will remain the same.

Hope to hear from you again soon. I'll try to call you soon. Take care and God bless you.

Love,   Joe (N.M)

next Joe sent Dot a Valentines card and it went like this.

Dear Dottie you make my heart sing! Happy Valentine's day! Hope you got the last package I sent?!!!Whenever I get my boxes unpacked, I'll get you some more nice things made! Take care and hope to talk to you soon!!!!! Love ,   Your friend Joe

This will be the final correspondence from Joe

Dear Dottie,

I really don't know just where to begin. I got your sweet letter and lovely photo today. I'll cherish them forever. There's something real here. There really is.

If a kid gets a crush on his teacher it's common from time to time. The say the kid is too adolescent to know what he wants. But I'm no kid. I've been an adult for many years but in your eyes I might still be a kid to you. I've always been attracted to older women all my life, but usually in the age range of 10 to 25 years older than myself. When I was 21 I was engaged to a lady 57. When I was 26 I dated a lady of 58.   We dated became engaged and were best friends for 12 years. I never married these women because of outside complications (through no fault of mine) . I dated since, but I never found anyone yet that I cared for as much as either of those two ladies. I'm sorry to say they have both passed on. But then you came along by coincidence or perhaps fate but you thrill me (so to speak in the same way they did) I knew they were much older than me but they had a special youthfulness about them and a special sophistication like no one else I ever met. You have this too.

I mean how many women over 60 or 70 are going to pose in a negligee, perched on the hood of a car outside???? (another drawn smiley face). Most women your age wouldn't have the courage and some wouldn't have the ability to get up there and down again. Ha! and also you have the body and shape and youthful skin of a young model!!!! Could you be a real life Auntie Mame? I'm financially comfortable, and will inherit one third of Texas someday so money is not all that important to me. I've always been around it and in it. Yet if you and I got together people would talk and say I was after your money. I really don't care what anyone would say. I've been the brunt of gossip before but I don't know if you could handle it or not.

Dottie (love your name) I really don't know you but I really care. Your're so unique. I'd be proud to be in your company. Your family would say you were crazy and mine would feel the same way about me. But I don't care if you don't.

I've been looking for real love all my life. The kind that comes from the heart but so far the only love I've found sincerely is the kind that comes when you open up a fat wallet (mine). But I really don't feel you care whether I had a dime or not. I feel you care just because I'm me. Is this true? To me happiness is not measured by the time spent. Instead it's the quality of the time spent. I'm a warm, very gentle, tender, very generous, very affectionate and loving man. I have a heart as big as the universe. I treat a lady as a queen and there aren't never have been very many young queens. (smiley face) But a person is as young or old as they feel. I'm an honest , respectable, Christian businessman. I don't lust after women , but the little things are what meant the most to me. Like the super feeling I got when I received your letter and photo to think you care knowing I'm alot younger. The other things that would be special to me would be meeting you in person for the first time. Embracing you, holding your hand, kissing your hands, seeing you smile at me,walking with you, talking with you, being with you alone or in a crowd. Serenading you on my guitar, being near you in the moonlight, knowing you care. Evidently, from what you said in your letter you are not age conscious like most people. Of course I haven't told you my age yet either. Well nothing ventured nothing gained. I'm a very mature 40. And you are a very young 76. So that makes us about even as I see it. What about you.? Of course I haven't asked you to marry me. All I've asked for is your friendship and what does age have to do with that? (smiley face). But I would like to be a special friend. The kind that can send you gifts without upsetting you , or making you feel guilty or cornered. And I'm hoping you will be the kind of special friend who accepts my gifts with a smile and wears them and uses them. And remember I do it from my heart and there are no strings attached. You have my promise here in writing. Do you believe in Fairy Tales? The kind you read about in books and see on T.V.? Well, I do, I believe in happy endings too. Call me a dreamer, or whatever you want, but I believe love is where you find it and keeping it alive is a daily task.

You said you'd be my Valentin e. May I also be your knight in shining armor and slay all your dragons. Your prince charming. Dottie I've never said this about anyone else but regardless of all the pain, heartaches, trials and tribulations I've had in my life they've all been worth it. I'd do it all over the same if I had to just to meet you.

Although I may give you alot I ask for little in return, just your special friendship. I would be so honored if you find me worthy of being yhour close friend.

Sincerely, respectfully and with much love,   Joe (N.M)

p.s. Enclosed is a recent photo. I'm going to call you (not knowing the best time) and hope I don't put you in an embarassing way with your family if they answer an d ask questions later. I don't ever want to hurt you in anyway. My sun sign is Sagittarius (November 23 rd. The best female friend I ever had till now was also a Taurus - May 19 th. God bless and take care. Please let me hear from you soon (telephone number included here with the notation "call collect") Please call in case I don't get you when I call. If my housekeeper answers ask for me. Thank you so very much for just being you! Your great! Love Joe

I asked Dot what ever happened here . She told me when she got the picture and saw his bushy beard she decided to cut off all correspondence.

Dottie Zimmerman

Oh sweet mystery of life.

This next trilogy of corrospondence was from an ad Dot responded. The ad went like this . ORE. Very alert, big band musician, 83 still playing, seeking woman 70-80, young at heart, funny, caring, nondrinker. Photo, phone

12-9-96
Dear Dorothy,
Well, thought I would answer on your blank letter head herein.
I am born May 28, 1913 Glendale N. Y. 5' 7" 155 lbs. auburn hair, no glasses have about three beers month if that much . Smoke very little quit once but started to get heavy so went back to it. I lived New Port Richey for 12 years. Came here four years ago. Kids said dad what if something goes wrong your 3,200 miles away. What will we do ? So for their sakes I am again here but miss New Port Richey very much.
I was with Ted Lewis for 3 and a half years. Have his album signed to me by him of "Me and My Shadow". Also my good friend Kitty Kallen sent me her big hit "Little Things Mean Alot" autographed also. She just called me a few weeks ago telling me her husband passed away suddenly. Quite a blow to her. They were planning a come back but now I do not know but she will let me know soon. Was even on prime time with Kitty when I still lived in Florida. I am also past exhaulted ruler of Elks and life member, past worthy president of Eagles, life member of K C , belong to Moose not active, American Legion Post 104, and natch musicians union.
Photo took May 28th. 1996 my birthday bash where I was playing. Gave me a nice cake too. Had to go show proof to them they did not believe I was 83. Thought I was only in my seventies, how about that.
Incidently I live with my oldest daughter here since I moved back here four years ago on command of the kids. They said if I had someone living with me there in Florida they would of not worried that much, huh.
I was in Sarasota a few times when I lived down there . Barnum and Bailey's museum was kinda nice.
Well drop me a line please. Let me know your ups and downs what other info on me is needed. And one thing for sure if it's God's will so it will be so set tight and who knows how things will end up. By the way I like bowling. I also go to bingo with couple friends of mine twice week. god bless hope to hear from you again if not best luck.

Musically yours,Chuck (OR.) My little toy fox terrier says hi too woof, woof huh

still Chuck12-22-96
Dear Dorothy:
Thanks much for your very nice letter and also to learn of your kids. where they work etc.. Sounds like you have a very good family but as I said whatever God has in store for me so it will be. I said I will be honest with you and as of the moment I am waiting on replies to other entries I received. Got a couple so far only one of them appeal to me and you on my list too, but time will tell what's what again with God's will.

You know the name Zimmerman was a personal friend of mine . His name Jack Zimmerman and he was planning on getting married. Was rushing too much furniture etc. out of his apartment. He keeled over and that was that. Only 72 years old always did follow my band wherever we played. He was one darn good dancer but loved my latin songs more than anything. He certainly could do a Samba plus waltzed around the room like Marie and Gower Champion whom I worked with lots.

Maybe you heard of the Gowers. They were in movies too, They felt badly when my ex did what she did to me. We were years ago at their home in St. Albans Long Island , sometime in the year of 1955. Unfortunately they both passed on now.

Just like month ago my very good friend Kitty Kallen lost her hubby too . Just got a call from her a couple of weeks ago. She might start a come back. Hope she does she sings great for my money. Have you heard of her? One of her golden records was "Little Things Mean Alot". I have not only her picture but her album of "Little Things" autographed to me. Also one from the great Perry Como was at his home in Jupiter in 1978 for dinner. Frankly I miss Florida. Loved the climate. Loved going crabbing much there too.

Well I chewed about enuf fat for now. Say hi to your kids if we ever meet warn them. I am awful tease that's my life. I love making everyone happy, that's entertainment right!

Have a merry christmas and a happy new year, stay sober. I do not like drunks huh see ya who knows it's possible.

Musically yoursChuck (OR.) Have you got another photo. Please, thanks

49

Dottie Zimmerman

2-7-97

Dear Dorothy:

First of all sorry about the delay in writing you but as you no doubt heard we got hit here with bad flooding and I lost alot including all mails I received   let alone photos etc so if you could please send me photo although beauty means in no way anything to me with those replies. It's just that I kinda would like to see what kind person is involved with me.

No I have not forgot you nor any of the others whom were kind enough to answer that ad.   But again if it's to be God's will whomever so it will be, right?

I might say now if your seeking man with lots of do ra me what things stand now I am in no way that lucky. Thank God for my S. S. and the little extra I make playing here. And to top it off no insurances to cover our losses here too. Never did . We think anyway this kind of act of God would never happen here.

As for me healthwise I was suppose to go to surgery wednesday Feb. 5th but it's all cleared up. I had a bad case of bleeding hemmroids. Got a few injections plus using bag balm. It's cleared emensily so I cancelled surgery. They were going to tie off the worst using rubber bands but there is nothing terrible then that I heard, so again thank God it's all gone now.

True too I missed that lovely Florida weather you make me sad mentioning too. Oh well who knows maybe I might get to feel it all again, but there I go just dreaming I suppose.

I want to get this off today so perhaps by Tuesday you will receive this. Please drop a line at once again photo if you can. Reminding you I seek a big heart not the prettiest of a gal. With warmest regards. Also from Dolly woof, woof, I will sign off. Looking for your letter shortly please.

Musically yours, with loveChuck (OR.)

Dot never did get anymore replies from her letters. She figured he either died or ran off with Kitty Kallen who as at this time has not made any comeback I've heard of.

1-4-86

Dearest Dorothy,

Thank you very much for answering my ad. Your letter reveals a person of depth, compassion, affection, inner warmth and the essence of

50

womanhood.

Please excuse any things wrong with the writing. I'm just becoming use to the computer. I am 41, a school administrator, highly educated and successful. As I look internally, I wonder if people of that combination have it harder than others as ego seems to stick out and makes it more difficult to get in harmony with the spirit that governs the world. I have two boys, Daniel 16 and Matthew 14 who make their dad proud. I came to Ethiopia in January 1985 after having started my teaching career here at 22 with stips in between in Wisconsin ,New York, New Jersey, Taiwan, Nebraske, Texas, and California. So my roots are varied but not very deep.

I consider myself extremely tolerant, gentle, affectionate and sensuous. I believe the most beautiful creature of God is woman, woman and femininty in all it's varities. I have come to the conclusion that we're all here searching for our meaning and purpose and that the polarity and opposite beauth and attractiviness of the sexes should teach us that many of our answers are contained in the union, both spiritual and sexual of the sexes, that making love is an act far beyond the biological and pleasure act that most describe it as, that it is a quest for oneness, wholeness, healing and meaning.

I, unfortunately had a deprived youth in terms of role models in love, affection and sensuality. I have tried to compensate eversince. I have discovered through the concepts of Cazza, Tantra, and Tao that by denying my immediate sexual and physical pleasure, I can imibue my lover with a beauty unmatched and reach a peace, compassion and love for all that transcends the everyday world, that tells me that there is a loving, non-judgemental creator that is not interested in laws, man-made morality, sin, guilt, and other rationalized actions, but only in acts of love performed selflessly.

As you can read, I'm frank and not into trivia. I believa that letters afford us the opportunity to reveal ourselves painlessly. I believe these letters should do one of two things. Either decide that our interests are not compatable or get to a point that we fall into each others arms as soon as we meet.

I will be throughout the states for at least two months this summer and I can easily come to you if we have reached the latter or second goak, a goal I hope that we can quickly reach. Please write soon and enclose various pictures, if possible. I can only send this one for now as developing pictures is very difficult in this country.

Love,Hal (Ethiopia)

5-12-88

My dear ms. Florida,

Just received my Globe magazine of May the 17th and saw your wonderful advertisment in ti which so impressed me that it forced me to write you. There is so much to write but will wait until I hear from you but will tell you a little about me. Like you I am also 75 years of age a lonely widower, my wife died of cancer in 1969. We had 3 sons and a daughter, my oldest son and daughter also died, at present I live alone . My house is paid for, i am in pretty good health. I have a 1986 Ford Escort but only a two seater. I am religious as well as lovable and caring, everything you could ask for and expect, I must say, living alone is no fun and in looking back I will admit is what prompted me to write you. I gave you my address and here is my phone number. I am asking you to please call me as soon as possible and reverse the changes, in my heart I feel we were made for each other. I beg of you, please don't dissappoint me.

Love,Charles (MD.)

The next 6 letters are from the same Charles. Here goes!

6-27-88

Dearest Dottie,

Well my dear another day is passed and no letter or word from you . I pray that by this time you got my letter and pictures, believe me my love, I think of you often with writing you and always looking in the mailbox for a letter from you. May I ask what did your son say when I called Sunday? I am so glad that you were home each time I called. I pray that with all your admirers you chose me. I'll tell you again, I am so lonely, living alone. I applied for residents at 2 retirement homes here in Maryland but what they are asking it was too high for me. They wanted about $1400.00 per month. It was too much for me. I don't believe I told you of my religion. I was raised as a Luthern my wife was a Italian Catholic but we weren't married catholic. What is your religion and your nationality? For me my mother was German decent and my father was English decent, I am writing this letter to having something to do which will bring us closer, may I ask how far do you live from Tampa or New Port Richy , Florida.

A fellow I worked with on the railroad here in Maryland took his pension and moved to Florida. Well my love I now must stop for now but I pray I do hear from you real soon.

Love 4-ever-n-everCharles (M.D.)

6-19-88
Dearest Dotti,
As I told you on the phone here is the letter and pictures I promised yhou. I am so happy my letter to you through Sheela Wood got through but I am most happy I had the chance to talk to you. I wasn't kidding when I told you, you looked about 45 years of age, by the way my enclosed pictures were taken in December on a bus trip to Wilmington, Del. May I tell you, you write the sweetest letters and when you said, I love you on the telephone that was the first time I heard that for a long time. It seems so funny that when I ran a train out of Phila into Harrisburg I passed the town you lived in never thinking I would meet someone from there. Praying you and I can make a happy life for each other, it means so much you say you are a one man woman. Well my dear I am glad to hear that as I don't want to play second fiddle to anyone as you may have suspected as we get closer to knowing each other. I want to be the only one in your heart. Thought I told you but maybe I didn't I have one son who lives in Canada with his wife and four children and works for the U.S. government and another son who lives in Maryland who works for the fire department has a wife and daughter. You speak of your ancestors my mother was of German decent and my father was of English decent. What a small world this is. I too have alot of stories and troubles to talk about but being we just ment and being that I am still upset about our meeting like this I suppose It can wait.

7-2-88
Dearest Dottie,
Received your letter the other day. A little slow in answering because my son and his family was in from Canada. He has four children which keeps me busy when they are here. I wish to thank you for all the kind words you wrote about me. Even though we never met. Feel as though we knew each other for a long time, speaking of the weather, it is nice and cool here, it has been for about 2 weeks now. Pray your daughter and her friends enjoyed their selves. What I meant by second fiddle is that I want

a one man woman and I agree with you. There is alot of things to consider. I want you to be happy, also it is best not to rush into anything. We would be sorry for later so we will play it by ear for awhile and I don't blame yhou for not wanting to live up this way again. Glad to hear I am not alone as you used the name Charles often, I would not know if our sun signs are compatable. I never gave it much thought like you and I want to be agreeable with you. I too would like to write to each other and try to work things out, I am most sure we can, my son and his family visit me over the 4th. of July. He is the one who lives inCanada and he has four children they really kept me on my toes as I am not use to being around alot of children any more. I will be glad when this holiday is over with that I will close but before I do, I will ask you to please write soon.

7-8-88

Dearest Dotti,

Received your fourth of July letter and I must say with every letter I receive from you I find a new way to get to you. As you said that Port Richy and Tampa are only 50 miles from you, I just saw my friend from down there so I am not planning to go south anymore this year but will start to figure out a way to visit you about this time next year. You are so right when you said it's hot, the same here, that suggestion about going to Hawaii sounds good to me. That's another thing going for us. My son from Canada was here to attend a weddsing but when he left he only got about 15 miles from here and his van broke down so he had to stay one more day until he got the van fixed. He had to get a new radiator. It's a good thing it happened not too far from here. It was about 2 years ago that I saw the Niagra Falls for the first time, due to lack of time I didn't fly over the falls or did I take pictures but it was something to see, when I go to Tampa to see my friend perhaps i could stop and see your son also and make myself known. I am Luthern also but like you I don't go to church as often as I should with all this trash about religion it makes you disgusted. It is my ipioion to beleive in God and worship in your own way you'll be alright. Yes my deak I like jokes and I like the kind that makes you laugh. Yes we do need rain but from what I hear and read you are getting more rain then we are getting here up north. Yes my dear I do have flowers around my house, mostly roses. I believe I got all your letters . We all have to wait until the post office are ready to deliver then or any other part of the government. Yes my dear I will do as you suggest,

I will call and take my chances. Well my dear, I really don't know if I have much more to write about so I will sign off for now, please write soon as I love to hear from you and look for the phone to ring as I will call you soon

7-20-88

Dearest Dottie,

You are so right when you said that this is a hot day and I can't understand why it stays hot so long which brings my up to the reason I didn't answer your letter of July the 9th. before this. It is even too hot to write or even eat but about another month or so we will be looking for some of this hot weather. It is very true that it is good to see friends and relatives sometimes but it 's alot of work when they go. My son from Canada was here and hais van broke down and he had to stay a little longer until he had it fixed. As for you going shopping with Lorraine don't spend all your money save some for a rainy day. You are as bad as I as where you live you have to have a car to get anywhere or you walk. It is about 9 miles to the citgy and stores from where I live, good for Les doing all that work and I mean it's work. That's one good thing being on pension, work is a thing of the past. All those birthdays are over by now until next year. It is a little late but happy birthday to all. As for that leaf you sent me, may I tell you I put it between the pages of my bible. We can't raise trees here like you can in the south. I do have a magnolia tree and it is growing hope it don't die. Those gardenia plants do smell good like you. I am going to stop writing and get this letter in the box before the mail woman gets here, closing with love and please write soon.

8-11-88

Dearest Dottie,

I was really surprised to talk to you last night, yes my dear I have been sick since I received your latest letter and while sick I was thinking of you and what I had on my mind to tell you. First with all this hot weather and your telling me you woudl never leave Florida along with my age, home and property I really don't see any sense in carrying on like this. I am afraid that if I plan on anything it will not work out so I guess all this was a big mistake. So sorry if I dissappointed you..

Love 4-ever-n-everCharles (M.D.)

The next 9 letters are letters from thesame man. They go exactly like this

4-14-87

Dear Dottie,

Thanks for writing. What paper did you find my name in? I have not placed an ad since July 1979. I'm 70 (9-27-16). A oving Libra man. Live in 2 bedroom home on a lake since I retired at 75. I go to warmer climate in winter. Have spent one in Fl. (near Ocala) , 5 in California, 2 this past one in Las Vegas.

5' 7" - 180 - Blue - gray/blond - ruddy complexion. V ery healthy, active and virle. Do not smoke drink or drug. No medication except vitamins.

Fish and swim, dive and drive, travel, T.V., music (all but hard rock), movies and theater,

Born in Columbia, Mo. Graduated high school 35 and business college 36.

Worked in hotel and restaurant business until I enlisted in 41. Was tail gunner on B-24 with 8th. and 9th. A.F. . Shot down a POW, 16 months. Reinlisted in 47 and served in the Korean War.

Worked in various corporations till I retired at 78.

Married briefly 45 and 46, No children. Married 62 - 71, Three beautiful kids. Michael 23 lives in Ca. Patrick 21 just married lives KC. Teri 20 spouse and 3 yr. old daughter liv e in KC.

Enough this time tell me about you and ask questions.

I don't have any religious preference. Very seldom go to church, but I do believe in God. I pray, I meditate, at least 2 times daily. I'm a very fortunate man and I know it.

A very happy Easter to you. I like your photo. You have legs. I'm definitely a leg and breast man. Just fixing to leave for a week to 10 days. Will be going to Bronson Mo. and there across to KY & TN. Hope to have a letter waiting when I return.

A New FriendChurk (MO.)

P.S. address to Chuck, there is another Chas L. on this route with very close Box No.

4-24-87

Dear Dottie,

Old Mark Twain sure knew what he was talking about when he said: "If your don't like MO. weather, just stick around a minute, it will change" I arrived in MO, from Vegas, on March 8. We had beautiful warm weather for a week then 3 wks of almost continuous rain. Then a week to 10 days of freezing temp & snow flurries. Sunday (Easter) & Monday, it was in 90's. Now we have cool 40's, nights and 60's during day.

I'm going fishing this pm, come hell or high water. Have only been out one time for an hour. Nothing. I do love to fish, even though, only for sport. I can't eat them.

The silicone would not scare me away, though I might forget and take a little nibble of the wrong one. I have made love to a woman with a single masectomy and am corrosponding with a lady who had a double.. I also knew another lady , now married, who had a Dr. that wanted to remove her breast, she consulted another M.D. and each time had the non-malignant lump removed and still had her breast.

Guess I had better explain. I too love the water and have nice boat rides, whether I catch anything or not. I do alot of my prayers and meditation when on water observing God's handiworfk.

I'm an alcoholic but have not had a drink of alcohol, nor any other mind altering drug since March 20, 1952. I'm also a very active member of Alcoholic's Anonymous. I go to alot of meetings and conventions all over USA & Canada.

I have a small Toyota mini botor home that I travel in. Own this place to stay here in summer only. Can't take the extreme cold anymore or, perhaps should say I don't have to.

I enjoyed winter of 80-81 near Ocala, Fl. I had friends AA who lived in Homossasos Springs. He is now deceased and she moved back to MO..

I can smell the perfume, what is it? Love it.

I also prefer big band music and love to dance, though I mainly stick to fast foxtrot now.

I spent Easter alone in KY. My alternator went out I did not get it repaired until 3 pm. Called my sis & told themn I could not make it. Ate at a Church's Chicken.

With SincerityChuck

7-10-81

Dear Dottie

We have been getting rain every day. Had 6 inches ov er 3rd and 4th.

My daughter , daughter in law and grandaughter have been here since yesterday. The boys are away.

I sometimes wake myself snoring. I have had sinus trouble for many years guess that is reason I snore.With both Lorraine and you there keeping house shouldn't be too much of a task but then there are the kids and that requires alot of extra work.How old is this gal Carol, who is a contortionish? She must still be fairly young, orf else has been doing these acrobatics all her life. I'll bet that Lorraine is good. My son studied photography for 2 yrs. in high school and one year in college but has never practiced it for other than personal pleasure.

I'm hungry you shouldn't be telling me about this good meal. I fixed swedish pancakes and scrambled eggs for breadfast. I had a beef stew in the crock pot for lunch.This evening we are all going to the Marina where they have live music tonight. I'll have to dance with all there.

Write -Love   Chuck (MO.)

7-29-87

Dear Dottie,

Sorry I'm so late answering was in KC at my daughters and then went to a family reunion. It has been hot. No rain since July 8th. Has rained all around here, but not right here. You must lead a very active life, sounds like something going on all the time.

I know what you mean about loving family but needing peace and quiet times also.

I do wish we could meet. However, don't know when or how. Right now I'm very busy with AA. I just keep getting asked to speak to help alot of new groups etc. Also we have 2 new state funded treatment centers near here. New people coming into the program everyday. There are 2 new ones right here in the sub division where I live.

My daughter and grandaughtedr were here over weekend. Also new daughter-in-law. My son worked again. I haven't fished since the 8th of July. Talked to some of the real diehard fishermen and it's too hot even for them.

I have a class reunion or picnic to go to in September. I don't usually watch TV in daytime but with this heat been watching some of the contra hearings. I also have been watching some of the early game shows just before news.

I wish I knew where I could go and find 65 - 70 degrees year round, not too dry not too humid weather year around. Dan Diego County DA. is about the best, but it's not perfect. Maybe some of the islands.

The B/D parties sound like fun but know as a lot of work for you two.

I bought an 82 Chevy S-10 truck so have reliable transportation.

Write - Love Chuck (MO.)

8-10-87

Dear Dottie,

Believe it or not we got just a little rain last night. First time since 8th. July. It wasn't much but will help. Our weather temperature soared last week. We hovered around 100 but never went over officially. However , mine here always registered more than the radio says.

I'm with you though. I try to put on a smiling face. It's no use crying. However, this is 2nd. straight year we had been having such high temperatures. I'm beginning to believe some of those old people who keep saying it is the astronaut's fault for messing around in the atmosphere.

I had AA friends during last weekend with 2 ten year old boys. I took them fishing early both Sat. & Sun. Total catch was 5 fish. Howev er I had some in freezer and they had more than enough to eat.

My daughter & friend came yesterday and are still in bed. We went to little beer joint and stayed until midnight. Boy you should have seen the heads turn whenever we walked in. I loved it. This girl works with my daughter as she is originall from MS. she was reluc tant to go out (she's black). Think she was enjoying it though. They watched a movie on the VCR after we returned. I went to bed and they are still in bed.Sounds like Shawn knows what is good in life. I have a counted crossstitch thing on my wall that reads "If you want to be happy for one day get intoxicated. If you want to be happy for 3 days get married If you want to be happy for 8 days kill your pig and eat it If you want to be happy for a lifetime learn to fish"

I'm with your son in trying to stamp out those perservatives. i try to buy natural foods as much as possible.

I know that dolphins would like to c ommunicate with us. I'm sure that they try everytime I went fighing there they went out too and were awaiting our return.

Dottie Zimmerman

Write, Love,Chuck (MO.)

8-24-87

Hi Dottie,

Boy this month is flying by too. It is only 61 degrees at 6 am. We have had rain and a cold front from Canada. I had to close door and sleep under a sheet last night.

If this keeps up for a couple of days I'll be back on the Lake. It's been nice since Sat. evening.

Mowed my front yard last evening and hope I can get rocks done today. However prediction is for rain. It probably will too. Always does during State Fair Week. Our fair is only 30 miles, not as good now since it is in competition with a Harness ractng. I may go up on seniors day and I can get in for one dollar. They used to have alot of large tents with all kinds of fine entertainment and food. The only ones I have heard about this year is Budweiser

I went over to my sons, 75 miles then another 45 to KC. Towed an old pinto for him. It wasn't a total loss, my daughter and grandaughter came by and we all went out for pizza for dinnjer. My grandaughter also has all kinds of dolls and stuffed animals. Everyone gives them to her. A friend of mine made her a raggedy ann and andy doll set. I think they are her favorites at this time.

The Gary Collins show must be local , have never heard of it. Nice that you can have an early dinner and then relax and visit and decide on evening pleasures. I have been going to alot of AA meetings. Went to 13 one week here and two other places.

I would loved to have seen that fashion show where they modeled their clothes for Goodwill.

Some of my kids and maybe all (in mo) that's two will be here this coming weekend. Patrick has promised to come and get my motorcycle running.

My favorite colors are green and blue. Have always liked green don't get to wear too much though. Can't really find suitable shirts in green. Don't wear ties much anymore. I had a mixture of green-blue (called Mediterranean)colored rooms in my home in KC. Sold house when I retired. If I was there I would wash your back whether you showered or bathed.

Got to get going. This house needs cleaning, bed changed etc.

Write, LoveChuck (MO.)

End of letters end of relationship

9-10-87
Dear Dottie,
Had a very good Labor Day weekend. Spent alot of time with daughter, son in law and my perfect granddaughter.

Then on tuesday I went to the VA. hospital and had my suspicions confirmed. I'm a boarderline diabetic. Have to monitor blood sugar twice daily. Take two 5 grain glyburicle tablets daily and of course watch diet and sugar intake. I can live with it. I have enough confidence to think my pancreas will start producing enough insulin again.

It is raining gently at 7 am. I had to reach for cover again last night. It was in the 50's and is in 70's during daytime. My son still hasn't been over to put my cycle together. Maybe this weekend. I talked to him on phone. If not he will be on vacation early October. I have been very active in AA, going to 6 meetings per week.Alot of people look for me when they are having any friction in their groups.

I like yellow, also on an attractive lady especially when the lady has a tan. I was taught white was not a color instead the absence of color. In art appreciation I think. Also like different colors on different type persons. Tourquoise or orange looks good on some. Then of course, there are bodies like you with almost a perfect body who look good in any color. My favorite picture of the ones you sent is the one in black. Your smile is just right in that one to fit the mood.

Went fishing boat with AA friend and had a good day. Lots of carp not too heavy big enough though.

At our annual "Monte Carlo Day" annual affair at AA club in KC I was a seventy-five dollar winner. It is a charity event and you are allowed to purchase overpriced merchandise only. I got a nice blender for me , new car stereo for son. VCR tape and game for daughter and grandaughter.

I wish you were here, this is type of day to be with a pleasing body of the opposite sex. I have one more 6 or 8 day trips into Illinois, then I'm through with speaking circuit for summer
    write Love Chuch

P.S. Reread your last letter and opened this to answer. Have watched Oprah but don't make a habit of watching daytime T.V.. Heard of her in the "Color Purple". Love chocolate however it doesn't like me. Have not had it for years and now it's out. I don't know that I have ever deliberitly had garlic dressing and cayenne red perrer on toast. I take a garlic and parsley vitamin at night. Also A and E take at lunch.

9-26-87

Hi Dottie,

I'm not too worried about bloodsugar. It is a nuisance but I should have been on a diet anyway. I have every hope that it will be stabalized and my pancrease will start producing enough insulin soon.

Your grandaughter is a very nice looking young lady. Thank you for sharing photo..

Patrick and Mary (son's spouse) are to come next week. e will put the cycle back together. It has been sitting since 1973 gas in tank and water rusted. Had the tires relined. The motorcycle only has 28 miles on it. Thanks for the birthday card and the clipping. I thought Les was the one into protesting nuclear radiation.

You, nor your daughter will be able to do anything for Shawn until he acquires a desire to stop drinking. When that occurs please support him and his AA activities. Tell Lorraine to join Alanon and Christine could join Alateen when she is a teen.

It is 11:30 am I just came in and will try to get this in mail. Sheusually gets by early on Saturday. Our weather is really ideal and fishing should get good. Patrick is an avid fisherman and maybe I taught him too well. Last time he caught 7 bass and I was 0. I'm ready this time.

Speaking of fish. We are having an AA fish fry at the state park tomorrow. Expect 150 people at least. Had over 100 last year. I don't eat fish. Shawn mayh have to start over a number of times, it is hard for a 20 yr. old to admit to a drinking problem. I was 35 when I went to AA. It took the first time. I have not had a drink since March 20, 1952. However it's still One Day at a Time.

My My meetings ae not coming to an end I'm just not going on anymore speaking trips this summer. I will continue to make 3 or meetings a week.

Go to KC on Monday. I have to be at VA hospital at 7:45 am Tuesday. Hope my condition is stable enough to get checked for new glasses. I am wearing old ones. They are O.K. for closeup but upper is not satisfactory in artificial light. You are right about me being crazy for my one and only grandchild. She is something else. She is v ery sharp for a 3 yr. old and is very curious about everything. Wants to learn, try to put her in pre-school 2 days a week this past summer.

Write, LoveChuck (MO.)

10-17-87

Dear Dottie,

Thanks for pin and necklace. My grandaughter Natalie will love them. You really lived an exciting and active life. I don't think you have even been able to finish a letter without interruptions.

My son, wife and her girlfriend came Wed. Then another AA friend and fihsing buddy came. We three fished Thurs. am. until water got too rough. I was only one who caught any. Got only two yesterday. It rained all day and we mostly watched movies on VCR . I love having them however they leave half filled glasses of coke etc. all over the house. Lights and baseboard heat on etc. You know how that is I'm sure.

Am sorry Shawn did not stick with AA. Maybe he will go back. We have a saying about AA running ones drinking. That sounds like a great type vocation for two guys or any two people. Now if there were just fishing holes between those motels or lodges.

Our trees are most all turned beautiful expecially the Maples. You can really see them out on the lake. We all forgot to take camera Thursday. The kids are leaving this am. Going to KCV and Worlds of Fun. Patrick is going back to work Monday am.

My checkup VA on 13th was superb. They cut my pill intake again. Am only taking half per day now. After tomorrow only have to monitor bloodsugar 3 times weekly. Hope to control it soon by diet alone.

I will be leaving around 26th if my bills all come in and that lady comes through with my house payment.

Will go to La first and visit my other son Michael. Will not arrive at Las Vegas until 2nd. or 3rd. week of November. Do want to spend Thanksgiving with my neice and son.

My AA friends want me to stay until after halloween. Some are having a costume haloween party. would love to see but it is really pretty too cold for me.

Yesterday between rain squalls Patrick and I fished . Only caught small whites and carp.

I may try to visit with my son Michael over xmas and new years otherwise will spend wice neice in Vegas

Write, LoveChuck (MO.)

Here is some of Dot's letters that I've grouped in batches to the best of my ability. Just bear in mind that no matter how sweet it looks on paper it just never worked out.

12-21-87

Hi Darling,

It looks like lovely Dottie would write this old lonely Tennessee hillbilly and tell me about herself. I carry that picture next to my heart and hope. I will b e 73 March 28. When is your birthday? I went in the army 1941 in air corp. made Sgt. and I spent 2 years in England, France and Germany. I was discharged in 1945 and went to work for Eastman Kodak and before that I was a policeman in Va. for 2 yrs. and a railroad cop in Va. for a year. I have been divorced 12 years and have a pretty little apt.. Two bedroom sleep in one and keep one just for junk, bugle and so forth. I worked at the VFW on weeksends at night. Worked all the dances. I started in 1965. I was the bouncer dude. Guess I could bounce a rubbedr ball now.

I have 5 children, 2 boys , 3 girls youngest girl is 20. All the rest married. I have never been to Florida and hope to one of these days.

I'm sending you two more pictures and if you don't like them tear them up. Hope you will write if you need a stamp holler.Ha! Ha!

Love and kisses, Big Lou (TN.)

Please I hope you can read this as I want to hear from you

Hi Darling

How is pretty little Florida gal? I appreciate your writing to me but please don't faint because I won't be around with the smelling salts. First of all I had a nice house and could of sold it when the ex was 62. House worth about 40 thousand but decided to let her live there if she pays the taxes, sucker. I have 5 children t6wo boys and three girls none came to see my but my oldest boy. I have been divorced 12 years. I lost the hearing in my left ear but I can hear gairly good in my right ear over the

64

phone. I forgot to tell you I think I'm 6' 6" tall and weigh 215 lbs. I get a fairly good pension $1025 a month but the way things go it about takes it all. I have a 20 year old daughter that wrecked car and she had two drinks and they arrest her D.W.I. and it cost me about $600. to get her out of it. Then my ex wife took her to hospital and used my visa and other card and put &1900 on it, the other card is a Mastercard. I have two years college but you can't recogn ize it from this letter. The daughter had cancer and they said they cured it and it won't come back. Well my beautiful lady in Florida will close for now..

Please write,Big Lou (TN.)

1-10-88

Hi honey,

I received your letter and I was sure glad to hear from you. Have you heard that song, I want a rubbedr dollie to call my own. I would rather have the real Dottie. I have that lovely picture of you and wish I had one to carry in my wallet. I don't go home anymore even for Christmas. They stick me with a $1900 hospital bill. They put on my visa card and master card. When I got my bill from visa this month they said I hap paid $1225 interest last year. My ex didn't get all the house she got half of it and I could have sold it when she was 62 but like a dope I let her and my daughter live there as long as they pay the taxes. I stuck my neck out on charge plates. My ex came over here the first she ever came to see me. I said you got trouble haven't you. She said yes and said my daughter had female trouble and took my cards to Atlanta Ga. and put $1900 on them . I found out she had cancer and they were sure it wouldn't come back. I'm not sorry b ut it takes about 5 years to pay them off. My picture was awful. You should have tore it up. If you need another stamp please holler.

80 women answer that ad but Dottie is my favorite and I sure hope she will answer this letter. I have never been to Fla. and who knows I might go. I get $1050 a month and want to go somewhere this summer.

Love you,   Big Lou (TN.)

Next here are three letters from a 39 year old man who was one of Dottie's admirers.

Dottie Zimmerman

12-27-89
St. Pete Hi!
How are you? I got your name by Single Keeper Club. First let me introduce myself. My name is Tret "m 39 years old, 5' 7" tall, 135 lbs., have a black hair, brown eyes, I'm a single man, never have been married. I work for a wholesale supply and I'm a repair technician. I likes music, movies, dancing, beach, outdoor and I'm clean , honest, sincere, understanding, warm, gentle.

The reason why I writing you because I believe you are sincere honest, compassionate and understanding. I know you have had a hard time in life like myself, but if you are thinking to have someone special in life then we are both have to take a chance with each other and give love and friendship a second chance and if you also believe that to have someone special is greatest and highest level of happiness then we must open our hearts once again.

For the simple things in life I enjoy most of a nice evening. Candle light dinning. Sitting by a very special one while I embrace someone really nice. Someone like you. I also enjoy kissing , touching and making love and feeling that wonderful and warm sensation of intimacy, it nice to have someone to share with. I'm not hard to please. It's nice to go to fine restaurant or staying at home watching T.V. while someone snuggled next to me. If you are interested in me please write to me and hopefully we both can get together and become the best of friends ever more. Hope to hear from you really soon.

Your new friend, T.P.(Fl.)
p.s. If you like to call me call me at..............................

12-27-89
Hi!
How are you? I have your name by single's club. First let me introduce myself. My name is Trent, I'm 39 years old, 5' 7" tall, 135 lbs., have a black hair, brown eyes,. I'm a single man have no children. I'm working for pool and patio and I'm a repair technician. (may I interject here - even though I'm only the typist I really never though there was much calling for technicians to repair pools and patios, - just an observation). I likes music, movies, scenic drives, like collecting coins and antiques and I'm clean, honest, sincere, understanding homebody. Warm and gentle, don't do drugs.

The reason I writing you because I believe you're compassionate, understanding, honest and sincere. I know you work hard in life and have had a hard time but if you're believe that being in love is happy in life then we're both have to take a chance with each other and if you also believe that being to have someone special and share life with is greatest and highest level of hapiness then we must open our hearts once again and give love a second chance. We must never give up our pursuit and right to be happy.

As an Asia man I was born and raised in small town and I'm very loving , faithful, caring, and trustworthy. For the simple things in life I enjoy most of a nice evening candle light dining sitting with someone special, while I embrace someone really nice, someon e like you. I also enjoy kissing, trouching, making love and feeling that wonderful in life it's nice to have someoned to share with. I'm not hard to please, it's nice to go to fine restaurants or travel, staying home watching T.V. while someone snuggled next to me. If you're interested in me please write to me or call...(phone #). Hopefully we're both can get together and become the best of friend, lover or even a permanent parft of my life. I'll be ever so proud! Hope to hear from you soon.

Sincerely,Trent (Fl.)

p.s. call me at 5:30 p.m. If you like (phone#)

Trent must of sent out the same letter to every letter he answered because then next letter to Dot by Trent is exactly the same as the previous two so I see no need to type it out. So much for the Trent a thon. Now on to another set of 3 letters by a man named Bud.

10-7-89

Hi Dottie,

You answered my ad in the Globe yesterday. I got a package of about 50 letters. I imagine that they wait till they have alot to save on the postage.

I don't smoke, drink or do drugs. My birthdate is Nov. 22, 1924. I am a scorpio on the cusp. I like to hug, pat, kiss as I was brought up in a loving house.

I have two grown sons in MO. , 3 grand children and 2 sisters, they all live in MO. Older women who dress in shorts are nice to look at. I am enclosing a photo. It is a copy of my pass port from Jan 89.

I do live quite a way from you. I did live in Clearwater, Naples and I spent a month at Siesta Key just out of Sarasota.

Write me a longer letter and a photo please.

Bud (Fl.)

10-21-89

Hi Dottie,

You should have told me how beautiful you are and those long legs. You really do look sexy and yes I smelled the scent of your perdume and I liked it.

Our weather turned cold and windy Friday and it was in the 60's today is not so bad as the wind has died down.

The reason that I live in Fl. is that after my divorce which was very painful for me but it had tgo happen, I literally ran away from home. I had spent a lot of time in Fl. and I had liked it and I don't like cold weather. I live in a mobile home about 8 miles to the beach and about 10 miles to the everglades. I moved here in 83 and have been here ever since. I am 5' 8", 185. I was an oil jobber with a string of service stations in Mo. Of my passport, the time on it had ran out and I had to renew it . Prior to that I have been all over Europe and England. I go to the Bahama's about ever other month. I have no secrets either and we both need to feel free to ask or say anything as that is the only way we can get to know each other.

I like C & W also blues but no opera either. I may go to a halloween party that I am invited to. As you know I am a scorpio on the cusp. I am a kisser, patter, hand holder and yes I enjoy sex with the right person , one that I feel is right for me.

Looking at your photo I feel that you may be the right one and I may make a trip to you in November. How do you feel about that!!

Love ya, Bud (FL.)

10-29-89

Dear Dottie,

Actually I would prefer to stay in a motel as it would make me uncomfortable to stay in a house with your son and his family. I would be coming to see you and get acquainted with you so I would not want to spend alot of time visiting your family. I am thinking of around Nov. 5th. or 6th.. How does that suit you?

I am going to a halloween party tonight dressed as the devil.

Bud (FL.)

amongst the letters there were 2 postcards from a man named Don. They were both sent from Toronto , Canada. Both were dated Sept. 17, 1988. This is what they said.

Wanted to send those from Toronot (his postcards I'm assuming) but I did not have your address with me, late, but better than never   Don

Spent a few days here looking around. Visiting several interesting sites. Leaving in a few hours for home.   Sincerely,   Don

Here's a couple more from an Ohioan

6-17-88

Dear Fl 9190L,

Saw your ad in the Globe thought I would answer and see if you would care to exchange photos and phone numbers. I have sent out photo and some do not care to return but I assure you I will answer your questions and correspond with you. I am 70 years old weight 165 , 5 ft. 9 salt and pepper hair . I am terribly lonesome and would like to hear from you. If you are interested I will tell you more.

Edgar,(OH.)   Phone #

6-30-88

well Dottie,

Will answer your letter and return your photo so your 76 just a number. I'm 71 so what you look beautiful so it's no matter what's your age. Yes when I come to Fla. I'll try to contact you but it won't be for awhile yet as far as I know but if I do I'll try and find a place near Sarasota and if your not married we'll see what we can have together. I have been to Sarasota many times a beautiful city. There's alot of rich people retired there. I generally find a place to rent somewhere for the winter down there right now it's plenty hot enough up here for me we need rain bad.

I don't smoke or drink either but I can drink a beer once in a blue moon but I couldn't stand a smoker. I am a retired stationary engineer. I put 10 years at tool making and 25 yrs. at steam engineer for state of Ohio. I have a pension with SSI and one from the state of Ohio about 900 per month not much but I get by. I live by myself raised a family on a farm there all gone my wife dead from cancer. Well like you said if you stay single I'll contact you later.

Love,Edgar (OH.)

So much for Edgar now onto George.

1-24-85

Dear Dorothy,

I noticed your nice photo in Photo Album magazine and since we both live here in Fl. I decided to write. Enclosed is my picture. I stand 5' 8" and weigh 160# have brown hair and blue eyes. I have been divorced for 6 yrs. and I'm 62.

I love all sports especially golf, which I play. I do not smoke but like to drink a moderate amount of beer. Drugs are unknown to me. I hope you will answer my letter and send a picture.

Maybe if we have a correspondence we can arrange a meeting, which I think would be exciting.

Hoping to hear from you soon.

Yours   George (FL.)

2-6-85

Dear Dorothy,

Thank you very much for answering my letter and especially for the cute sexy picture! I wish you would send me more like that!

Honey, I do not even consider our age difference, because "age" is a state of mind. I've known people 60 yrs. old and they look and act 80. But I've also known people 70 who look and act 50. We are both the same sign. I'm also a Taurus. Born on May 8, 1922 in Boston , Ma.. I'm also English and part (50%) Irish. I don't know if it's good or bad that we're both Taurus but if it's bad we'll just have to change it. I'm glad you don't smoke and very glad you like to drink beer that means we could have alot of fun together. I think it would be really exciting to meet you and I hope we can get together soon. Apparently you are tall and slender (at 5' 7" and 135 lbs.). I would really like to take some pictures of you at a pool or the beach. I like your silver gray hair. Is it soft? By the way, the perfume on your letter is terrific!

Yes I would like to correspond with you, and we really don't live too far apart, so I hope we can have a personal meeting soon. Speaking of correspondence, my 1st. letter to you was returned because I addressed it to 22nd. St. . I almost threw it away but at the last moment I checked to see if I had addressed it wrong and of course I did, So I re-mailed it and I'm so glad I did. You might be interested to know that I wrote to 5 women in that magazine. Truthfully I did it out of curiosity! But on the other hand, if I met someone, and all systems were go I would carry it to whatever level we mutually wanted. In other words, I want to be honest with you. I'm not campaigning for a one night stand, or a live-in arrangement or a marriage.

So I have to tell you up front that everything would depend on just how you and I relate to each other. By the way in the case of the other 4 women, only two are writing to me. One wanted to come here and live with me immediately and the other asked me to send her $20 for some nude pictures. But I believe your letter and your photos, are much more quality. (Besides, I love you in a shawl and feathers). I keep looking at your picture and I'm going to put it in the corner of my bedroom mirror...(a place of honor)! Honey, I hope you will write again soon.

AffectionatelyGeorge (Fl.)

2-13-85

Dear Dorothy,

Thanks again for another nice reply. I'm like you, I like to write when it's quiet and no distractions. It sounds as if you're one big happy family there.. and that's really nice when you can all get along so well and you have alot of companionship so you don't get lonesome and depressed. Also, all the activity is good therapy and I'm sure you enjoy it all. I have been to Philadelphia, spent a few weekends there. Mostly because my roommate at Yale lived in a fashionable suburb , but I cannot remember the name of it now. All I remember is they had a fabulous night life and many, many bars.

You asked me if I am retired. Yes, I took an early retirement last June. I am not wealthy, but on the other hand I didn't need to work anymore. I was an insurance salesman. I would like very much to meet you sometime. Of course I don't know how much freedom you have, so I don't know what to suggest. I live here in an apartment of my own, but I don't dare to invite you over for a weekend because then you'll think I only want to go to bed with you, and so there goes our correspondence and relationship. Anyway you can think about it and let me know How, when, and where? I would like to take you out to dinner and then go dancing. I think it would be fun and certainly exciting!

By the way I vacationed one year on Siesta Key. I rented a beautiful home right on the beach from a couple that were going up to N.D. for 2 weeks. It was near a par-3 golf course that I played several times during that period.

Hope to hear from you again soon, and can't you get your daughter to take some more cute pictures of you or do I have to go over there and do it myself?

Affectionately,George (FL.)

on the envelope which contained these three letters Dottie wrote "not good for me" so I guess that was that.

5-19-86

Dear Dorothy,

Here is a picture I just took today. All I can say is honey if you dress like you did in this one picture you would soon find out just how much tender loving care that you can take. I hope that it would be such fun that you would want to stay around and keep getting pleasure and TLC everyday.

Love,Lou(Fl.)

6-2-86

Dear Dorothy,

I've started writing dear John letters to some of the answers I got. I just told one gal that she had too many other things to do to have time to keep me happy. That I didn't want someone that was never at home.

You sounded like you are more my type. Someone that enjoys doing things for and with her man. No always on the go without him. Not the type that would say not tonight dear I have a headache, "but if it feels good let's try it again". One little thing dear please leave off the perfume. It turns me off. No dear I didn't dream of you last night but I am day dreaming right now. Thinking of how nice it would be to hold you and kiss you until I pet you with desire. So your 74 well my dear, I'm 73 and if you wore that little sexy outfit around me we would soon find out if those sexy ideas were all in your head. If there were any juices of life left in that old body.

Love,Lou (Fl.)

I guess Dot didn't like the crack about no perfume cause there were no more letters.

5-22-87

Dear friend,

Thank you so much for answering my ad. It was very kind of you. I never expected to receive so many answers to my ad. In fact, I received so many I could not answer them all personally, but I do want to acknowledge each and everyone. So I thought this would be the best way possible.

Again thank you for taking the time out and answering my ad.

Sincerely,Sam(KA.)

12-20-85

Dear Dorothy,

(Someone I'd like to know)

Your listing in (Queens Photo Album) caught my eye and I thought that you would be very interesting to know and also m eet.

I like the description of you - your age of 73 also your height of 5' 7" tall but like very much your weight of 130lbs. this is all just super.

Yes Dorothy your size also your age would be the kind of woman I like to get acquainted with. As for me I'm a retired veteran fianacially secure with good income. I own my home and car. I'm of German and Polish discent and a widower as my wife about 12 years ago died of terminal cancer. I'm 63 years old I was born on January 20, 1922 and I'm 5' 8" tall and about 175 lbs..

The things I enjoy doing are fishing, camping, traveling, photography, but also like home life and country western music. I'm a bit shy but very affectionate, loving and romantic (I do not smoke or drink).

Seeing your listing and the description of you I just can't resist wanting to know more about you. would like very much to correspond with you and we can tell each other all of it. I will tell you more after I hear from you.

Amxiously waiting for an answer, Good night,Sam (KA.)

p.s. I have children but all are married and living away from home. I will enclose a photo of myself in my next letter and I would also like a photo of you.

1-23-86
My Dear Dorothy,
Many thanks for answering my letter. When I received it I couldn't open it fast enough. I was so glad you had answered it. And now I hope you don't stop writing me as I'm very interested in you Dorothy.

Yes I agree 12 years is a long time to be a widower and it gets awful lonely at times. I just have not found that special one. I'm of German and Polish decent. I was born at Hillsboro , Kansas about 60 miles from Wichita but I've lived here in Wichita about 35 years now. Since my wife died and my children gone I now live here all alone. Like I said it sure gets lonely.

I ws married during World War 2 while in military service in Europe. She was from Ireland and we were married in England. She died 12 years ago. I have 8 children 5 are boys and 3 are girls. All are living away from home. I also have 22 grand children. I have 4 brothers and one sister.

The things I enjoy doing are fishing, camping, traveling, photography , dining out. I like taking walks, holding hands in the vovies, but also like romantic evenings at home. Music I like country and western.

I can see by your letter that you could have a very romantic spirit inside you that is very warm and inviting. I know I would be very anxious to know you in person. Yes your letter attracts me to you very much.

I"m enclosing a full length photo of myself. I do hope you will like it. When you write ask me any questions you would like to know. I shall say good-night until I hear from you again. (Very anxious to hear from you again).

Love ,Sam (KA.)

p.s. I would like a full length photo of you.

2-26-86
My Dear Dorothy,
You have been constantly on my mind so I just couldn't resist a letter to you and I do owe you a letter. I received your letter with the photo also the valentine with a letter. thanks so much. I must admit I like the way you write and also the photo I have of you Dorothy. It is my hope that in

time we can meet and really get to know each other. That is of course with your permission.

I'm alone here with you in my thoughts. I read over and over thed letters you have wrote. I'm honest with my feelings and frank in telling this to you although we are still like strangers to each other and miles away but when I think of you as if you are very near and have already seen you.

However it is enough to make my heart jump with the thought of us if we meet. I have your photo here by my bed so I can see it all the time also see you the first thing in the morning. I now have special thoughts of you. I'm sure that we would have much to offer each other. I'll close and say good night and think of you in my very special way.

With much love, Sam (KA.)

I found no more written letters but he did send Dot an Easter Card, a Valentine's Day Card, a St. Patricks Day Card and a Christmas Card.

Dot answered this ad(Active white male 85, financially secure, seeks senior lady to share townhouse apartment, rewarding relationship. Would consider relocating to Fla. or Ga. Photo, letter, phone) on May 27, 1992. Here is a letter she received from Sigurd

6-12-92
Dear Dorothy,
This is in answer to your letter of May 27th. I sure do appreciate the answer to the ad I had placed with Sheela. Thank you.

This is my second trip with placing ads in Globe for a much needed partner in life. In 1977 I met a lady through Sheela and we did get married in the fall of 1977. However it did not exactly last. She got a divorce just lately and we parted still friends. However it was a clean break and no harm done.

Now and then I find myself quite alone in this world and do wish to alter that if possible. That is the reason for me trying to find a lady who might tolerate me.

Your letter bothers me somewhat in that I get the idea that you need to be with other people and be entertained quite a bit. I am enclosing a photo taken with my former wife. She done took most all of the pictures that we had during our 15 years together so I wouled appreciate if you will please return this photo since it happens to be the only picture have of my former wife. I am returning your photo in case you want it to send to some other person.

I do like what I see in your letter so I would appreciate a little info. Do you live in a house? Apartment? Who with? What do you do , work?? Do you have an adequate income to take care of yourself? Do you drive a car? Do you have a car of your own? My ad stated I want someone to share my apartment, how about that? Maybe you got to stay in Sarasota? I have been through there a number of times on the way to Naples. We used to go there quite often. Gimmie an answer and then we can go from there. Might be fun. Let's see what happens.

Incidently my typing is a farce. The signature is from a stamp I had made years ago. Account I do have a case of Parken son disease. Handwriting is out of the question with me. Hope for the best . I still play golf.

Gby for now Honey, C ya.First name is Sigurd (GA.)

9-18-92

Hi Dorothy,

Was surprised to receive a letter so close so possibly we can meet in the near future. I have lived here in Tampa for 23 years but it's getting worse every day so soon I am planning on selling my house and moving somewhere it's quiet.

I have been to Sarasota quite a number of times so don't have too much trouble finding an address.

I don't know of much to say so if still interested write and let me know. Will close for now.

Sincerely, Dale (FL.)

by the way Dale's ad went exactly like this.

Fla. White male, 68 (looks 58), 5' 11", 185 lbs. grayish-blond hair, blue eyes, home owner, nonsmoker, social drinker, likes C&W music, camping, gardening. Looking for lady for permanent commitment. Age, nationality unimportant. Can relocate. Photo.

Now let us continue with the only other letter I can find from Dale.

10-6-92

Hi Dorothy,

Received your letter a few days ago and am just getting around to answering.

I may be in Sarasota this Saturday afternoon so if so will be sure and call. The other Saturday I had to go to Coco Beach and exchange a welder for some piping so didn't get to come your way. I don't know of much to say so will close and hoping to see you soon.

Sincerely,Dale (FL.)

We can only assume that meeting was not magic.

Next we have a rare look at a reply and a response from Dorothy. It was a one hit wonder.

3-29-88

Hello Dottie Dear,

Got your letter I think you are nice looking and you do write a nice letter. You answered all questions most honest and your size fits my order to a tea especially after looking at your picture and reading your letter. I can tell you have class . I don't think I can afford a woman of your class . You said that that car was yours. Some car if I'm any judge of a car that's a new cadillac. I can't afford a new cadillac on my income. What is your monthly income? I'm sending you some pictures. If you don't like what you see and read you can send them back and I will send yours back.

p.s. I'm sending you a clip out of the paper that's why I don't like big towns. Live Oak is about half way between Jacksonville and Tallahassee. 400 miles from you.

Buford (FL.)

now here's Dot's reply

3-31-88

Dear Buford,

Received your letter today. Let me compliment you. I like your picture. Why did you have it taken in a store? Glad you liked mine. No offence, but I am sending yours back. I don't think you would care to move here, Sarasota. I love it here. Believe me I am affordable. I shop at thrift stores and am very good at it. I know good things and I do dress well and like to look nice , but I am far from rich. I sure hope you were kidding about me buying you a cadillac. My social security is very small and my son c annot afford a cadillac. He works very hard for everythings he gets. I agree this world is really getting crazy. You have to be very careful when choosing friends. Maybe you can find a good one who would and could afford to buy you that cadillac. There are many wealthy women in Florida and I really wish you the best and I have nothing to offer but me. I hope you hav e a wonderful Easter and happiness always.

Your friend,Dottie

Old Buford sent Dot back her letter. At the bottom of the letter he wrote. "Thanks dear you can't blame me for trying. You look so good in the picture. Bye Sweetie , Buford.

On the side of the envelope Dot wrote "Maybe you can buy me a Cadillac!"

Forward March!

2-1-89

Hello Dottie,

I received a list of ladys and were looking it over and I saw your name after reading over what you had said seems like we both look at life the same way. I liked your description so decided to write you and see if you would care to correspond and get to know each other. Will giv e you a description of myself. I am in my late eightys in very good health. I am 6' , 165lbs., brown graying hair, blue eyes. I believe in cleanliness. I dress neat when I go out. I don't smoke or drink or use drugs. I do not have any children or pets . I am retired. I like baseball, fishing and T.V. news or good programs and country music. I like to have flowers and some tomatoes. I don't have space for a big garden. Keep my yard looking nice. I drive and I go any place I like to find a companion that would be compatible for I like to take trips to see different things and do what we both enjoy. I am enclosing a picture so you can see what I look like. So will close and not bore you.

Sincerely,Guy (AL.)

2-14-89

Dearest Dottie,

Received your nice letter glad you answered my letter and we can become good friends. It sounds like you are a fine person and would make a good companion and not be lonesome for I like small ladies and I also like sex for it is good for a person. Nothing more enjoyable than to cuddle up and make love. Yes I like Florida . I used to live there and when the tourist season is over I will come see you. That is the only way to see if we would suit each other. Yes I have been married twice. My sign is Leo but you never said what you thought of my looks in the picture. Would you send me one of you. I am going to ask you some questions. Hope you don't mind. Do you have any children and grand children and are you a good cook. I do like good food at home , home cooked. I cook for myself. I do not dance and don't care for big crowds. I am a home man. Glad you like country music , do you like to fish for sheep head and would go to lakeworth at one time when I had alot of friends at lakeworth. I will answer any questions you would care to ask me . My life is an open book. So will close and be waiting for a letter from you   Be careful and stay sweet.

Guy

2-27-89

Hello Honey,

Will answer your sweet letter and thanks for sending me the picture . You are a nice looking lady. Just the right size. Wanted to hug the picture, you don't look your age.

Thank you for answering my questions. I like for you to smell good. I am a Major retired from the Air Force. My first wife died we had been married forty years. The second lost her mind and died within 10 months. The last one I divorced. I will be eighty-nine in July. Glad you like older men. I have a suggestion. Why don't you come up here and you can see if you would considerf relocating and we could be together. We could talk and get acquainted and see if we like each other enough to consider getting together. I have a three bedroom house with two bathrooms all electric. So you would have your own bathroom. I will pay your airfare both ways and you can stay two weeks and maybe we can decide what we want to do. I will lay my cards on the table and you can do the same. It is very lonesome living all alone. I am looking at your picture and if you were here in person I would hold you in my arms for you are just the size I want. I get too tired looking at four walls and when I go to bed my pillow has no arms. This is a picture of my house.

Do you think you could learn to drive by having one of them instructors teach you and show what to do. I know several ladys that were older then you that made good drivers. Do you have a phone? If you do give me the number so I can call you. It is a nice day here but it has been cold down to twenty. Since I have been here it has never been below thirty. So will close before I bore you to death and am falling in love with you.

Gary ((AL.)

3-13-89
Hi Honey,
Will answer your sweet letter and thanks for the nice card. What you said about coming up here suits me fine. Easter will just be another day. I have three sisters in Tenn. so I always go see them on Mothers Day so I will be gone for 10 or 12 days. When I get back we can get together. Why I asked you to come up here is so we can be together for I hate motels. Food not good and have to get dressed up just to eat a meal. We will eat out some, we can go to bed when we want and get up when we want to get up. We had three days of cold weather last week down below freezing . Cold killed all my azales and hurt the fruit and early garden. My nephew and wife came today. They have been in Florida for two months on their way back to Birmingham they have a big motor home will stay until Wednesday. I'm glad they came by . Good day.

With Love,Guy (AL.)

4-10-89
My Dear Honey,
I want to thank you for the lovely card , so sweet of you for thinking of me. I think of you more than you know. Sorry for being so slow in writing but I have been busy getting my yard and flowers and garden my tomatoes in order. It's good to be so cool at nights. I noticed today one plant had a bloom on it. I hope to have plenty of tomatoes when you come up. I want to get back from my trip by May the fifteenth. I will keep you informed on when to get ready for the trip to come up here. I am looking forward to meeting you for I believe we have alot in common. Maybe

when we get together we can make up for lost time. Will say goodnight and sweet dreams.

With love to my honey,Guy (AL.)

5-2-89

Hi Honey,

Nice to receive your letter. I enjoy your letters. Will be glad when I can meet you in person. I will start to Tenn. on Sunday the 30th. Will be gone for two weks maybe a day over two weeks. I will let you know when I get back. It is 8 miles from my house to airport and I will be waiting for you when you get off the plane and bring you to the house so you can get rested after the trip.

I do hope things work out for us for it is bad with no one to talk with and we both need some one to love. So I will keep you informed of any changes.

Love,Guy(AL.)

5-25-89

Dear Dottie,

Will drop you a note, hope you are O.K. I am fine enjoying being with my sisters. Nice weather up here warm days, cool nights good sleeping weather. Will leave in May for home. Not much news so will say good night.

With Love,Guy (AL.)

6-5-89

Dear,

I am back home had a bad trip. I was parked in my nephew's yard and a garbage truck backed into my car. It did twenty two hundred dollars damage. It took two weeks to get it fixed but I enjoyed seeing my sisters and nieces and nephews. I did some fishing.

Dottie I have thought alot about us getting together due to the difference in our age. Also you cannot drive and you have children that you love as a mother and grandmother. It would be hard for you to come here and live and not have your grand children around. I could not live with children the way they are raised now. If they are girls they drunk and pregnant and if they are boys they get on dope and want to come back to mother to take care of them. so far as your looks you suit me as I do not like fat women and due to my age I don't think I should get married. Just find someone who needs a home to come here and live and at my death leave her a nice income to live on. I wish we could of gotten together for I could of loved you. We could of went on trips and done things we both would of enjoyed doing together. I hope you will not be mad at me for I plan on coming to Orlando to visit and I could come by and meet you and I could stay there for two or three days. May I keep your picture if not I will return it. Good night and be friends with me.

With Love, Guy (AL.)

6-16-89
Dearest Dottie,
I will answer your nice sweet and understanding letter. I enjoying your letters very much for you are such a nice person. Only wish we could get together for you are the type of person I like and when I get down to see you and get to know you we might work out a way so we could get to be companions. I really enjoy your friendship and like very much and I would not hurt you in any way nor will I tell you a lie. I believe in truth and I had to tell you how I felt about you for you are the type I want. And I love you and would take care of you. I cannot see you at present, what time I will go to Orlando. I have some property I am selling so I don't know when it will sell. If it don't sell by Sept. I will come to see you in September for I want to meet you and family and really get to know you.

My phone # is......... Send your phone #. I will bring my camera so we can take some pictures together but most of all I want to see you in person. We are having alot of rain, hurting my tomatoes. Honey I will say goodnight. A kiss for I love you so keep sweet.

Love, Guy(AL.)

8-21-89
Dear Dottie,
I regret that I have to write you this letter and tell you about myself. For I think it is my duty to tell you. For I think you are a loving person and the type that I would be just looking for. I had to go to the doctor and I had him give me an exam. This is what he told me he said at my age I could never make love with a woman so how I could ask a woman to love me in my condition. I hope you will not get mad at me for telling the

truth. Sex alone won't make happiness but it helps for I have always enjoyed sex. I hope we can still be friends and I hope you can find someone that can give you joy. May God Bless and watch over you.

Guy (AL.)

And that was pretty much that. Throw in a few Hallmarks and Guy is a wrap.

6-20-91

Hi Pretty Lady,

I am not much of a letter writer but here goes.

I believe that I have the qualities that you are looking for. Young at heart youthful 70's non smoker no diseases never had any no bad habits. I am a widower it was 16 years last month since my wife passed away. Have been retired for eight years. Am looking for an honest, caring relationship based on love and trust. First best friends then who knows? I am not a rich man but I am comfortable and secure can relocate. Have car can travel anytime. Hope to hear from you soon. who knows what the future holds and there is so much that two people can do together if they are compatible.

Walk the beach in the sunlight and in the moonlight. Travel see all the sights, diance, flea market if you like that stuff. We can really do alot. Hope to hear from you soon.

God Bless, As always, Frank (OH.)

7-10-91

On the top of this letter is a newspaper clipping with Dot's horoscope which is Taurua it reads: Get better organized at work. A speculative venture could bring lasting financial security. Success depends upon strong public support, good timing and your own professionalism.

Dear Dorothy,

I was sure glad to hear from you, your letter was most welcome. It could be my lucky day when I answered your ad. And that picture of you!! How did you stay single so long??? You do look good enough to eat and you do sound for real. I am sure that you have heard of Budget Rent a car. Well I was Budget Rent a car ofEuclid Ohio. After my wife passed away and my kids grew up I sold out that was eight years ago. I have been doing some traveling but what hurts is to come back to an empty house. The house had 4 bedrooms it was a big house. And seeing I was away alot and no one could care for it I decided to sell it. It sold fast and now I bought a smaller place but still the same old story no one to come home to.

You do sound like a real winner and I can't wait to see you in person and who knows what a little hug and kiss can do to a couple of lonely people that have waited the storm out all these years. I am glad that you and I are being so honest with each other it will be helpful when we meet. It's been 17 years May 18, 1991 since my wife died she had cnacer and it was a tumor on the brain, impossible to operate on.

Anyway she never suffered. Eight months after it showed up on the x-ray she was gone. Had 3 girls and one son to raise. Well we made it O.K. none of the children ever were in trouble they all married and are on their own. So here I am on my own too. Pisces is my sun sign. I hope they are compatible?? You can ask me anything you want and I will answer them all as truthfully as I can so go right on and ask me I like that. There is alot I want to ask you but I thought I would wait until we exchanged a couple of letters. I didn't want to seem too bold since we really don't know each other. B ut I do love your letter and that picture of you. The picture don't do you any justice can't wait to get up close to you. Will send you a picture in the next letter and see if you still feel the same the next letter should tell. I am5' 6" tall 165# and salt and pepper hair anyway what's left of it. Hope you find everything I wrote helpful and that your feelings are still kicking in. Take good care of yourself and as always will be in touch.

Love,Frank (OH.)

7-22-91

Dear Dorothy,

What a weekend with nothing to do sure wished you were here or I was with you in Florida. There are so many things that we can do together and stay up all night if that's what it takes to get all the answers out. I feel that I have known you a long time and it would feel so right to take you in my arms and kiss and kiss you until we were out of breath. I sure hope you feel the same. That picture of you I love. You look so sexy on the hood of that car all alone. Wish we were together at either your place or mine. I believe that we could have a beautiful lasting relationship. As far as distance goes it's not that far we can work something out as how to get together soon. I am sure that I wrote something about myself such as I am in good health, very active and disease free want to liv e my life to it's fullest with a loving mate after all these years alone. I think that we should be together and that we would really hit it off. What do you think? "yes" Well I don't want to put it all down in the first letter or two will write more later. I am a non smoker do drink a little beer or a glass of wine now and then just a social drinker have not made a habit of it. Love to take walks and can just see myself holding your hand as we walk hand and hand together. Do you live near a beach? Thta's a good place to start walks from. I bet you spend alot of time in the sun and do you like to travel? I do know that you are a youthful petite clean woman and like all women there is something special you like to do. Write and tell me whatever comes to your mind. I am 5' 6 and a quarter" tall weigh 160 -168 lbs, that's tops very little fat. The scale this morning said 160. Well take good care of yourself. Write soon will send you a later picture real soon. As always will be in touch. Let's start to work on plans to see each other. Do you drive? I do Have car can travel.

Love,Frank(OH.)

7-24-91

Dear Dorothy,

Our letters are like ships passing in the night. I did send out a long letter with my picture yesterday and then I receive a letter from you today. I thought I had the inside track but things are not working out that way. I knew that you would get more letters and maybe a better deal who knows. I am sure that whatever happens will be for the best anyway I will just step aside for now and let you look over the field. Whatever you decide to do that will be your choice. I will just set my plans aside for now and sit this one out. You go ahead with your plans and I wish you all the good luck in the world. Hoping you won't get hurt just keep in touch and let me know when you run out of men. I did plan to come down in August. But I am not coming down to take you away from some other man. Take your time and let me know what happens. You can drop me a note and tell me to forget you. As always will be in touch. Do something nice for yourself today.

Frank (OH.)

Dottie Zimmerman

7-31-91

Dear Dorothy,

Received your card, letter and was very happy to hear from you. Honey first let me tell you a couple of things about running one of them ads. You are just like a kid in candyland. I know how you must of felt with all them letters coming at you. That is the way it goes there are alot of people that answer your ad and once you start writing to them they will go on and on putting you off. Then they start asking for money plane fare, bus fareor whatever there sick mother, brother needs an operation it goes on and on. All them letters you received maybe there was two or three that was special and they were sincere but you have to write and make sure that you want what he wants. You are putting the rest of your life into a stranger's hands. You say that it has been 12 years since your husband passed away. Now look back , how was them 12 years good? I am sure that you want the rest of your life to be as good and happy as you already have been. So what you do is write and answer and thank them and give no address so they can't write you back. The one or two or three that interest you that's the ones you keep in touch with. Then before you know it there will be just the one you want. And I am sorry that I misunderstood your letter. I do want to be the one and only one. There are alot of questions and answers that we both want from each other. I will just answer the ones you did ask me this time. No I was not in the service had my arm in a cast and flunked the service on account of my arm. Yes I do like to cook and if I must say so I think I do good. If I can eat my own cooking I know it is good. I am not the best dancer but I will get on the floor and be proud to hold you in my arms. I am sure that we will dance all night and get by and be happy with it. Would be honored to have a glass of beer with you. Now how does your son feel about you running this ad? I am sure that he knows. And how does he feel about you leaving? I would love to come down and meet you and see if we hit it off. If everything clicks no problem. I'm sure you will agree that first we should meet and court each other and see what are likes and dislikes are. If the chemistry is right we will know it soon enough.'THE HEAVENLY FEELING WILL BE THERE' I'm sure that you will feel it too. Will start to make plans to come down and see you in August. We will sure have alot to talk about and that's what we'll have to do get it all out. This card you sent me it's trying to tell me something. Whatever it is I hope it's good for the both of us.Take good care of yourself and keep up the letters will be in touch with you. I am sure that I would have no problem loving you. I do have pleasant sweet dreams of you.

Love,Frank (OH.)

8-2-91

Dear Dorothy,

Just a line or two to let you know that I am thinking of you. Everything is A O.K. up in Ohio. The weather is not bad at all but we could use some of that rain that you get everyday. Yes I am working on the leave town deal. Can't leave yesterday or today but real soon (Real Soon!!)   Can't wait until I can see you person to person one on one. Want to hold you tight and recapture that feeling that we are both seeking. Maybe this might be it and if it is we'll know right away. Take good care of yourself and do something nice for yourself today.

Love,Frank (OH.)

8-11-91

Dear Dorothy,

Honey is it all right to call you honey? Ask me some time why I ask if I could call you honey (honey story). Do you have a phone and what's the number?   This is personal what are your vital statistics "body measurements". Just want to know , curious. I know curiosity killed the cat but satisfaction brought it back. When it comes to food that's no problem , easy to please. Anything I cook I can eat and it is good. Too bad I was not there for your cook out. I love cook outs. Now you have me looking forward to seeing you eating breadsticks with that sexy look in you big beautiful lips. I do all the shopping as my son don't have time anyway I am the better shopper. I get more for my money. Now why do you people want to go to goodwill for bargains when you can get much better deals at garage sales?   Now that you ran out of space you and your daughter should have a garage sale and make a few bucks.   Well sleeping on a couch is not bad I am always falling asleep on mine, and if we have company from out of town I give my bed up and on the couch I go.

This place has 3 bedrooms and I have only lived here one year July 17th. 1991. My other home I had 27 years in it, had to sell it , my three married daughters, it just was too big to keep up. My son works 12 hours a day. Anyways it was a biggie, 4 bedroom 2 and a half baths two dining rooms a full basement front room and two rec rooms sitting on a piece of ground 200 ' deep by 300' wide. Could of raised cattle on it. All my children live within an hours drive of me. About how long I will stay down in Florida I have no answer at this time. First I have to get there and it won't be long from now. I did get ready to leave and then we had a deathe in the family. My grandchildren's grandmother died so that set me back about a week. Trust me believe me I want to see you in person just as badly as you want to see me.   Want to see how good you fit and feel in my arms when we hug. Yes I will drive down I know you need a car down there and if I stay a week or two no time table to worry about. I think of you everyday and I like the name Dorothy.   I never had a girlfriend named Dorothy. The only Dorothy I ever knew was on the wizard of oz over the rainbow. I sure did like that picture!! Well honey it's time to close one more letter or two and then I should be on my way down that is why I want your phone# so that when I get down near your place I can call just in case I get lost. You all take good care of yourselfs. All of you sound like good people and I am sure they will welcome any friend of yours. As you can expect the same up here. Do something nice for yourself today you deserve it. As always will be in touch.

Honey take good care,Frank (OH.)

8-8-90

Dear Dorothy,

Received your card letter today and as always can't wait to get your letter.   I am glad that your family knows that we are in touch with each other. It's no sin to meet this way. You say the other card had no message it was just a card. This card says on the back unlimited possibilities whatever that is it sounds good to me. Now you want to know how I stayed single for so long. Well to be truthful I really don't know. Had 4 kids to raise, one in collge 2 in high school and one in grade school. Had two businesses under one roof to take care of. I did take care of everything, didn't have time to think of marriage. I am very happy that you do want to keep in touch with me as I want to keep in touch and really get to know you. I do feel like I have known you a long time too and feel it would be O.K. when I see you to hug and kiss you that I would love. How do you feel about that? Well I will drive down soon it costs $250.00 round trip and one hundred dollars plus to rent a car for a week anyways. I think that's the way to go this time. Will be able to make it in two days so that isn't bad at all. I know where Sarasota is that is where the circus has it's winter quarters. When I asked if you lived close to Tampa I was thinking of another town. I have a friend who lives in Palmetto Mobil Home Park, Palmetto, Fl. that shouldn't be too far from you. The last time I visited them was about 4 years ago. How far is Palmetto from you? Almost in your backyard, yes? That birthday party sounded great, you did say you wished I was there well you can bet your blue booties I wish I was there too. Yes I came from a family of 6 my parents have passed away years ago and two of my brothers have gone to meet them. There are 3 men and one sister left. My sister lives in Chicago. She has lived there 50 yrs.. My two brothers live within one hour drive of each other. We kind of live in a triangle of each other. We do have get togethers all the time. Adults and the grandkids it's a ball. I am just an average fellow looking to live my life to the fullest with one good woman. You sound great! Like you say you can read between the lines and after all I don't know and yet after your first letter I didn't want anyone to hurt you. That whatever you want to call it is how I flet about you. And soon I will meet you then we will see if it's all there that we feel.

I have a Kodak disc and I am sure that we will take some pictures. Well honey take good care of yourself and do something good for yourself today. As always will be in touch Sweet dreams to you always,

Love, Frank (OH.)

8-30-91
Dear Dorothy,

Sorry that I have not wrote to you sooner. Just want to let you know that everything is A O.K.. Had to stop in Pearl, MS., to see a friend of mine who has been ill for quite awhile with cancer. Then after one day they passed away and I stayed until everything was calmed down. I am now in Florida about 2 hours drive away from you. Didn't want to just barge in on you. Want to know if I could come down and see you after the Labor Day weeken d. Must have your O.K., what I had planned was to see my sister-in-law and her husband for a couple of days and at the same time rest up a few days and come down to see you Sept. 7-8-9 whatever day you say it's O.K. to come down to see you. I am sure that you have wrote to me in Ohio but I did leave before receiving any letter. Anyway now that I am this close to you let me know what you want me to do. It shouldn't take more then two days for this letter to get to you and maybe 3 since Monday is Labor Day. Send your answer as soon as possible as I will be waiting for your reply. You can reach me at.................Tell me what you want me to do. Waiting, waiting and waiting

Love, Frank (OH.)

On the back of this final letter Dot wrote "came on Friday the 7th.". I guess the picture was worth a thousand words.

7-25-91

Hi Dottie,

Think you for ans. my letter. You wanted to no about me. am a widow of 6 years. I was born in Georiga, lived on a farm. moved to Tenn. lived ther untell 1951 came to Fl. lived in west palm beach 18 years but went back to Tenn. in the summer untell 1957 lived in gobesound narby 16 years. I lived in vacation moble home park. I have a 12" by 60" moble home det free. I live 5 children 4 in Fl. 15 gran children and 8 great gran children. I have 4 children in fl. 3 boys and one girl. one girl in Ten. I dont smoke or drink or use drugs. tell more about yourself and send me a photo of you if you have a phone send your number and i call you for i hate to write. I am seding you photo of me. you have hard last name to make out. If you answer again print it. i will have to past your adress my letter If you want to call me cleck. I am home most all day I go a fishing early in the morning to catch the cats some fish. Phone #...........

a Friend in Fl.Freeman (FL.)

8-2-91

Hi thire good looking.

How are you liking this hot wather. it sure is hot at Hobesound FLA. I hope your clost to Hobesound my name is Freeman and my hobby is fishing and walking the beach and picking up shells. and making things out of shells. I like to grow flowers . and to garden. and I like go on short tripts. I like c & w music and gospel music to. and I am in good health. I go every six months for a checkup and the nurse said I was healthy as horse. so much for that . an a widow for nearley six years. I hate I write I will clse for this time. I am sending my phone number.

Sincerely yours,Freeman (FL.)

Dot wrote on the envelope called him so I can only assume the conversation didn't go so well.

By the way just in case your thinking at this point that I'm the world's worst speller I've been deliberately leaving in all the cute and curious mistakes the letter writers have made. Es knot mi falt. U beleve that don't u?

11-16-91
DEAR DOTTIE:
I JUST FOUND YOUR NAME & A ADDRESS AND WILL WRITE YOU AFTER SOPPER SO IT WILL GO TOMARROW. I USED TO L LIVE IN PORT CHARLOTTE ABOJT L MEARS, SURE HATED TO LEAVE THERE BUT THRE HOUSE WAS FULL OF TERMITES SO I DID A LOT OF REPAIR WORK ON IT THEM SO LD IT THEN MOVED TO HOMOASSA SPRINGA FLORIDAAFTER $ HEARS THERE I EWAS ALONE BY THAT TIME AND I DID NIT NEED AS AS LZRGE A PLACE WHEN ALONE SO I SOLD AND MOVED TOTHE CNETER OF THE STATE AND BOUGHT 2 SMALL TRAILER AND XTAYED THER TWO YEATS AT EWHICH TIME A GOT MARRIED AND WENT TO GEORGIA .IVE WSITH MY WIFE . HER DAUGHTER & DAUGHTERS HUDSBAND GAVE SO MUCH TROUBL I WAS LUCK TO GET OUT OF IT. THE DAUGHTERS HUSBAND was ALWAYS , , KISSING & HUGGING HER. K SPOKE TO MY WIFE ABOUT IT BUT SHE DIDNT WA NT TO MA MAKE HIM QUIT SO SHE WAS TO INTERESTED IN A RENTER OF A TRAILER TOO. WHEN I WAS WORKING IN A BIG GARDEN HED WOULD BE VISITING MY WIFE.

SO I GOT TIRED OF IT ALL. I MARRIED AGAIN TO A LADY THE SAME AGE AX I WAS BUT SHE DIED A COUPLRR YEARS LZTER.SO IM GOING TO TRY IT AGAIN FOR THE TIME.THRE ONLY ONE THAT WAITHFUL TO ME DIED THE 7 of july 19/60

NOW IVE TOLD YOU MOST OF MY HISTORY AND I HAVENT EVEN SEEN YOU

or no LETTER FROM HER YOU FROM YOUR AD I LIKE WHAT I SEE. YOU ARE A WIDDOW, YOUR OPEN OPEN MINDED, BUT I EXPECT ILL HAVE A JOV BEFORE TO GET YOU

BECAUSE I USED TO BE   be 5 f ot 6 nc h es.   but h as ha v e swhrunk to APPROX 5 f t 8 . inches. MY DAD SHRANK 3 incfhes befre di h e4 deie4d. I AM KNOWN AS A CHECKER CHAMPION HAVIN WON THE   IOWA CHAMPIONSHIP   THE SPRING OF $& THEN MOVED TO WISCONSIN IN THE FALL 10 OF $& there was a blizzard in $* DAY OF TOURNEY BUT I ENTERED THE TOURN IN 49 aND WON IT a nde wom t h ru t ne nest 10 years althou th e record s a y s 8 times. hOW IT WAS t hey MADE A MISTAKE in counting   HO NOR POINT ******TS   aND GAVE THE CHAMPIONSHIP TO THE WRONG MAN AND SENT HIM TO PLAZUE TH THAT WENT WITH IT a nd i laqs t t TOURNEY TWO men f rom close NEIGHBORD WENT TO THEIR   ROOMS IN THE HOTEL   AND SAID THEY PLAYED TWO GAN+MES AND THE LESS STRONG PLAYER WON BOTH HAMES WHICH MADE HIM WINNER. BUT WE KN KNOW BEGAME BOTH GAMES TO A MA   COULD WIN ANYTIME   BUT HE THREW TH   GAMES HOPING IWOULD AGREE WITH THEM. I PUT THE   TPURNEY ON AND HATED TO TELL MY TOWN THET HSD SOME CROOKS +THE PUBLIC HAD DONATED $200   f or   the ri PRIZE FUND. SO I LET THEM GET AWAY WITH   AND THEY CREDITED ME WITH 2nde PLACE.IT WAS THE HARDEST THING I EVER DID bu t thery afre both dead no and I SAM STILL ALIVE.IF I HAD TAKEN IT WITH THE GROUP THEY WOUDS HAVE GIVEN ME THE WIN. AND GRANDE FATHER CLOCKS. I MADE   3   of THEM   I BOUGHT 3 of the BIG ONES BUT I MA MADE 2 OF THEM FROM thE   PICECES SAND I MADE THE #RD FROM SCRATCH i BOUGHT THE WOOD   AND MAE IT FROM THE BLUE PRINTS.I WISH I HAD THAT ONE BUT TWO LADIES WANTED   IT SO I SOLD IT.DO YOU HAVE YOUR OWN HOME IN FL FLORIDA/ HOW DO SPEND YOUR TIME/ COULD I SEE A SNAP SHOT OF YOU. only 120 pounds.THATS GREAT.   IF YOU HAVE A GARDEN I COULD BUSY MYSELF IN THAT. I LIKE TO TRAVEL, AND EAT OUT && HOLD HANDS AND KISS & HUG MY WIFE. IVE BEEN TO NEW YORK AND WEST TO THROUGH THE BLACK HILLS TO FT.COLLINS COLORADO THEN SOUTH   THEOUGH   NEW MESICO TO THE MEXIEEN LINE.   STAYED   ALL NIGHT INTEXAS BUT VISITED IN OLD MEXICO   THEN EAST   TO FLORIDA. I LIVED FLORIDA   ABOUT L* YEARS AND GEOTGIZ

@ YEARS BEFORE K CAME BACK TO THE WOMAN OF MY DREAMS DIED IN L(^) 1960 AND I AM TO BE BE BURIED AT HE HER SIDE WHEN I DIE. SHE IS IN THISTOWN OR NORTH OF TOWN A COUPLE MILES.THA REASON WHY I AM HERE. BUT I CAN MOVE AWAU AND CAN BE SHIPPED BACK WHEN I I HAVE # DAUGHTERS THAT, LOVE ME AND WILL SEE TO IT I GET SHIPPED BACK. I SPENT 19 years ma rried to her AND IF ANY ONE WILL BE SAVED SHE WILL BE ONE OF THEM. THAT YEARS WAS THE BEST IN MY LIFE.THERE ARE A FEW LWFT IF YOU CAN FIND THEM.MAYBE YOU WILL BE ONE OF THEM.IVE BEEN BOTHERED TIME AND ABAIN w3ile writing this letter so i dont know what i wrote. if you ask questuin ewill answer them/ a re you still 77? if so then i am 9 y ears older than wha.t is r ong with being 8 or 9 y ears o;der.MAYBE I WILL OUT LIVE YOU. I HAVE OUT LIVED MANY OF MY PEOPLE ALREADY AND I FEEL LIKE A KID. I EXPECT I WILL BE MAKING PRETTY GOOD MONEY FOR THE NEXT FEW MONTHS. ILL SEND YOU A PICTURE but they were not very close t i have 3 caqmeras and i get someone totake some more pretty soon then i will send you a closer up.I AM GOING TO GIVE YOU THE BALL NOW SO YOU CAN TEKL all AB OUT YOURself. WHAT YOU LIKE AND DIS LIKE AND MABY I COULD LOOK TALL IN YOUR TALL IN YOUR SIGHT. IT WONT BE LONG UNTILL YOU WILL BE 86 too. MAYBE I CAN MAKE THE NEXT FEW YEARS HYAPPY FOR YOU. IF YOU ARE HAPPY TH EN I WILL BE HAPPY TOO. I CANT WAIT UNTIL I HEAR FROM YOU? MAYBE MAYBE, MAYBE. IF YOU ARE NOT ALREADY MARRIED.

FOR NOW ILL WAIT. LOVE HOWARD (WIS.)

2-10-92

DEARCDO DORRIE

IVD HAD TOUR AD MZRKED FOR A PERSON TO WRITE TO AND I ADDWHO I CAN MARRY IF BOTH ARE SUOTABLE. THIS AD MAY BE OLD AND WOMRT HOW NOLD AFE YOU NOW THIS AS SAYS 77 COULS YOU BE 80 now? I SAM 96 nd goung strOND. BUT NED A LOVING LADY ro spend GOLDEN YRASGORIGETHER. I LIKE SAREA SOTA. HAVE BEEN RHTOUGH THERE MANY TIMES BUT LIVED AT PORT

Dottie Zimmerman

CHARLOTTEFOR 10 yeaRs   IF YOU AEW WELL WE CPULD HAV
E A NICE HARRIAGE YET. o amd ptrettu healthy   BUE HAD A
SVCALDED FOOT NIT I EXPEC R TO BE   WALKING SHORTLY.
MAYBE   I CAN PLAN Z TOUR RO OD PICTUREDS BUT HAVE
SOME   NOT SO GOOD AND WILL GIVE ONR OF THOSE THEN
WHEN ITS NICE OUTSIDE WILL TAKE MORE.EVERY THING IS
CCORD wIRH SNOW NOW.   IV HAD A PTETTY GOOD
EDUCATION and WOKBDKED HARD ALL MY LI LIFE.   ID JUST
DINE EVERT THING BUT WOUND UP DOUNG 17 yeard   in Resl
ESTAT   I LIKE SOME HUMOR   &IF MY WIFE IS HAPPY I AM
HAPPY.I KNOW THIS LIST NAY BE ILD AND YOU MIGHT BE
MARRJED ADREADT DO ILL ASK YOU TO ANSWER THID
LETTER AND IF YOU WOULS LIKE TO EXCHANGE A FEW
LETTERS THEN IF WE   BOTH FE FELLIKE GETTING MARRIED
WE WILL DO I.SO IF YOU STE FREE THEN STELL A BOUT
YOURSE; lf eha t YOU LIKE & EWHAT YOU DIS LIKE.
    SO WILL AWAIT YOUR LRTTERT.LOVE AND A BUNCH OF
KUSSRES.
    HOWATD (WIS.)

    p.s. A NICE PICTURE WOULSE BE NICE AND YOUR PHONE
NUMBRT
    This gentleman also sent a picture with heiroglyphs of unknown origin
on the back. Quite frankly it's too far out for me. Another impressive
point about the man was that one time he signed the letter Howard and the
other Howatd. Schizophrenia would explain that one.

    Here's a couple of new letters from yet another Howard. Unlike the
previous Howard these were readily decipherable. In fact this Howard is a
repeat. So here's Howard of Florida back for a second helping of Dot.

    11-4-91
    Dear Dottie,
    Some time ago I made contact with you , I don't remember the reason.
Anyway, I have dept the photo of you ever since and have often thought of
you.
    Time changes and so do people so you may not be interested anymore.
    I will be 61 on November 22, 5' 8 ", 190 pounds. I live in Davie about

275 miles from you but could drive to you.
Howard (FL.)

11-11-91
Dear Dottie,
I am enclosing a photo. FOOTNOTE FROM TYPIST (I remember the exact same photo). It's hard to find the right person but you can 't find one unless you look. Things I remember about you. You said that you lived with family so we would have to go to a motel but we never did make the trip. It's nice that you got alot of letters in response to your ad. I ran an ad once and got alot of letters but no real people.

God, that scent of your letter does make me horney. Do you put that all over your body? In a woman I seek clean, healthy, honest, loyal, non smoking, no drugs, passionate, loving, like to be loved, not into the bar scene.

Me, I'm a non smoker, non drinker, no drugs, like dining out, short trips. I also like you said I like alot of sex and I'm willing to do anything to please a clean lady.
Howard,(FL.)

I think that is the last letter from this particular Howard.

1-20-88
Classie Lady:
I hope that this letter reaches you in good health. I am doing better now! You may not even remember me because it has been so long since I wrote to you last. I am sorry but the Lord had other plans.

I had a business in Davie and another 58 miles in Belle Glade, but I could not get good help. Just when I thought I had Davie straightened out Belle Glade would fall apart and visa versa. Well to make a long story short, I fell asleep doing 80 mph. one night, mad because of another crisis and it was my fault and I am paying for it.

I broke my pelvis in five places, lost my knee cap, broke my back in three places and severed the optic nerve to my left eye. But the peovis has mended, cartgledge was placed over the knee joint with 115 stitches to show for it. I have a couple pinched nerves that have to be worked out in therapy but I will always be blind in my left eye. My scabs and scrapes have all healed and I have no scars on my face. I do have holes that they drilled through my legs to hold the traction on the bed. I am glad I wasn't older or I would have been in the hospital the rest of my life healing HA! HA!

Well , I don't have to worry about my business either. What was not borrowed by the un-payed employees, was taken by the landlord for non payment of ren t. My cars and trucks were sold by my lawyer to pay for the portion of the medical bill that was not covered by insurance and I still owe $18,000.00 balance and climbing with glasses, teeth and therapy.

If you think I'm kidding, I had received a roll of stamps for Christmas from my sister. With her quick thinking, and the help of her daughter they grabbed my 23 ft. trailer and hauled it to their place in Homosassa Springs. That's also where they hauled me.

They have been so nice, even though I have been unable to pay for anything, I did manage to go into town and get on food stamps and they even signed me up for some kind of energy refund due in March. I hate it when you have to beg for money and food No! No! don't get me wrong, they give me everything freely, but you know, the feeling you get when everyday they cook for you, clean and wash the clothes and even my body for awhile and yuou just can't help in any way. Well anyway, I have been very interprising in my life and have given more than a million dollars to three ex wives and still end up with enough money to get anything I want. But this time I am afraid it will take a little longer because of the back and trying to get used to seeing with one eye.

Anyway, I thought I would write because I have more time to do so now. That's if you wouldn't mind writing to me. I do so look forward to hearing from you but if you have indeed found someone else and don't return my letter, I will understand.Oh! I forgot to say, when they picked up my notorcycle and hauled it to the wrecking yard, it vanished! into thin air, and that was not even insured. Aren't people nice?

Anyway, I got my TV even though it is so far out here the TV is snowey, sometimes my neice rents a VCR tape for 99 cents or $2.50 depending on the day of the week and I get to watch it.

Anyway, I should close for now because I'm feeling tired.

Barbarajean, my sister is typing this for me as she said that I was making her sea sick writing on my side. CHUCKLE
Robin (FL.)

Yes, floor shows, thsie drinks, dinning in an atmospher created for those who can afford it...why not?...I knew, was taught not to have all my eggs in one basket...again a big BUT...We, I just was so envolved in Mutating of mink...I started in the 30's before colored mink...went thru the lucrtaive mutation dvelopement...it was great...my oldest son taak genetics, was a part of our mink ranch...and very rapidly...mink..short fur went out of style, plus the raipid growth....

Page ......2....I was taught if it cannot be said on one page not worth typing...You judge'

of the cat and dog business who ate the same foods, the production cost became prohibitive...That hurt, but I was mature enough not to lose my mind...so I have adjusted...with a modest self supporting SC check...My mobile home is close to everything...I can walk wherever I need to go including two large lakes...seperated with a narrow strip of land less then mile apart. So my fine mesh screened porch 10 by 30 is my living room...temperature permitting that is where I am...telephone, swivel rocker and truly comfortable ...especially since my life habits have changed dramatically...I can read, think, mediatate, wonder, dream and be realistic...My carport is attached to this porch it is 12 by 30...on the outer edge I have three tiers of hanging baskets...over 50 as I change them for new cuttings...my hobby...Beyond these baskets I have many other flowers..many types...On opposite side of my mobile I have over 20 rose bushes...In the back of this small lot I have a postage stamp size garden...gives my wonderful, fresh nutritious foods chemical free grown in deep organic compost...espallier type figs, grapes, pears and plums...So MY friend Dorthy...I am as busy as I care to be...Get many delicious meals in turn for driveing thse special ladies cars...I ask no charges... they tip me...feed me...so I have it made...and being absolutely a Gentleman...they have no qualms...Occassionaly years ago I made several trips...one waealthy New Yorker..upper state...visited her properties...we were gone three weeks...so I had a vacation...all in ine package...I love to drive..have Fl chauffeurs license...I had my own rig hauling cross country in my youth...I do occassionaly drive peoples cars...singles and couples to their northern homes and they fly me back...but this last year I have almost eliminated them...please not selfosh but only for those who tipped the best, stayed at the better places and did not mind the price of the better restaurants...so life is GREAT...I enjoy it immensely...BUT Dorothy I am alone...So will I find her or will she want me...that is the story...Yes Dorthy in our or my day I too enjoyed good Broadway plays...I saw them when in NY on business...Please I am human...I enjoyed the night life of Broadway...regardless of the night before...if on week end lay over I was in Collegete Church on Sunday morning...I am glad for emohatic Vincent Peale...who I enjyed hearing, now read his material...I know some sunk in deep, altho I was not aware of at the time...it is slowly seeping out now...I am so grateful...Yes I too one time enjoyed my Martinies...my Wild Turkey and Cutty on the rocks with water on the side...Yes we or the mink prosuers men I would be with went from one floor show to another...thinking how beautiful THEY we e...showing the most, wearing the least...of course the evening was never complete until we went to 8th. ave and saw the most graceful, beautiful bosies of the trained Belly Dancers (Greek)...BUT...I have been a part of IT...I thank God I always ran scarred...Deseases...in my pater life and pregnancy in my youth....I have abnormal health...I do everything to keep it that way...eating what I thuink aned k ow is best for my clean body...

Now how can I fit into your life...I am respecuful..know fairly well what people enjoy...in its place od course...always...I am not seeking a home...not material gains...wealth or being catered to...I have everything in my simple humble way of life...a radical change from my many years of worldly pleasures...I do not go to church...I enjoy some of the professional beggars ideas and philosophies...altho I do not always agree but food for thought...to desifer what I enjoy...TV sports, and news are my pleasure...not in a fanatic measure but pass time..I enjoy human health, talents abilities if in sports or any other shape or manner ..How is that?

This is getting long windeed..I awakened thinking of you...why write me, when you recognize I enjoy life...but differntly then ou..I love Fl...the casual wear...shorts whenever or almost all the time...I am not a looker or gazer...but I enjoy shapely women, in their shorts, their beautiful garments...You are 5 - 7"...I am 5--8"...180 pounds, heavy boned not fat...active and I surprize those who do not know my age...they think I am in the 60's...So please as to my abilities at this age...I cannot brag or prove anything...been a long time...just in case you are one of the type...who demands and seeks...what is human...I know the thoughts, the overall desires of so many...when driving their cars or their conversation with others they may have as guests...I get an inward kick out of hearing them talk after they have had more drinks then they normaly would have...so I get a kick out of life...people...yes women...So I placed the ad. I am getting many letters...so yours is one of the first to be answered...got it yesterday.

So please...I enjoy home life...beautiful music...doing what I can for those who appreciate...Yes I will enclose my picture again...you are the only one until I receive theirs...So your walking on the beach and the etc. might be intriguing...so if you have read this far, take it for its worth...one thing I am positive of...In no way am I selfish...I oblige to the best of what I can respect...so I am human, happy and might enjoy knowing you . I am just alone.

Merlin (FL.)

This whole previous letter is a mystery to us all.

9-18-85

My Dorothy,

You made me very happy when you answered my letter so quickly. Thank you so very much. The reason I write you is the age old reason. I want to hold you in my arms and love you to death.

You must remember one thing. One thing is very important. As long as one is beautiful one will always have men chasing you.

One day I will drive to Florida to see you. I hope you have enough room for me.

I will catch the bujs to Atlantic City this Saturday. Will send you a few post cards.

Yours truly,Ted(MD.)

9-27-85

My Dear Dorothy,

I had a nice time in Atlantic City this weekend. I won ten dollars. I fell 40,000 dollars short. I did buy a nice shirt at ceasar's palace. It would of been very nice if you were with me.

Love,Ted (MD.)

I guess Dottie just didn't have enough room for him.

9-19-85

This next letter was from a guy named Alfred who lived in New York City and dealt in rare books. He had all his flyers jammed inside the letter. On the envelope was a picture of what I suppose was him and on the inside he had another picture which looked totally different which I am sure is also supposed to be him. Just laying out the visual effects folks.

My Dear Dorothy,

I have seen your photo in Queen photo album. I am an Armenian 72 years old , 5' 11" , single. I like dancing , all sports. Please tell me all about yourself and Florida. I am a rare book dealer. I live near the United Nations. I am Jewish a good looking man. My telephone number is(phone#).

FOOTNOTE: By the looks of this letter he's several good looking men. Ha! Ha!

11-4-85

Dear Dorothy,

Saw your photo in the album. Thought I would drop you a note. Liked your description and liked it very much. I am 78, 6' blue eyes and brown hair beginning to get gray. I like sports and being outdoors. I have a car and drive. Am retired on Social Securfity. If you would care to write to me I will send you a photo an d tell you all about myself and answer any questions you may ask.

Very Sincerely,Don (VT.)

10-30-85

Dear Dorothy,

It looks like you have command of the situation in your photo. I don't know of anything I could say, only try to introduce myself. I have your photo and address through photo album. I am Johnny (he then gives his full name and address). 6 ' tall while and black and graying hair and brown eyes. Indian Dutch. So I like to play guitar and sing also. I like flea markets and the bible, I'm christian. I believe in telling it like it is. I hope you are not where all the rain and flooding is. You never know anymore. It has been raining here for the last couple of days.

This is not much but I enclosed a photo and would like one of you when it's convenient.

John (MO.)

10-12-85

Mrs. Zimmerman,

I am writing you , not because you are so beautiful but because beauty is an inner spirit that could be inspiring to a dreamer as I am. I was a bartender till semi-retirement . Before that I was a science writer . Live on the Ocean in Monthrey CA., Walk along area in Redwoods. I am Scottish, English, French ,German, 5' 8" 148 pounds. Could look at you forever.

John(CA.)

4-2-86

Dearest Dorothy,

Hi ! I have your letter and your very thoughtful card for Easter. I must apologize because I didn't send you a care. I've been alone so long and non one to send cards to that I became unaware of the holidays and they all became just another day to me, so please accept my belated wishes for Easter.

I can understand your hesitency writing someone you don't know. I only recently got the Queen album and when I saw your picture I was most taken with you. As far as knowing that you don't go to church it was in your description in the album. So it said you didn't go to church and liked to go to the beach so I am a stranger to you and I really want to know you. I have to tell you dear I have your note and your lovely card in front of me and your perfume you sprayed them with is driving me crazy -smile..and if we meet (and I hope we do) I hope you wear it all the time but I warn you , you can expect tender kisses wherever you are wearing it. I'm just a lonely single man who will be coming back to Florida soon, and I hope that I'll be coming to see you also as I really feel a deep feeling for you even though we haven't met yet.

I hope your Easter was a very good and nice one. Mine I spent alone as always. It was a beautiful day and I went to my favorite beach. You'll love it here as Cape Cod is all beaches, beautiful beaches. I wish you had been with me but I was alone except for my friends the seagulls. I go visit them about every day . They know my car and flock around before I even get there. If I walk on the beach they walk alone beside me like a puppy dog. I have a roll of film in the camera with pictures of me at the beach . As soon as they come back I'll send some to you. I want to be honest with you dear, I am a real and rugged man but I don't have my left leg. I lost my left leg while in Ocala befoer I moved back here so I'm in a wheelchair or crutches or a walker sometime. It don't stop me from doing anything. I do all my own things with no help. I am on the go all the time. I drive my own car , etc.. do all my own cleaning, cooking , sewing and I work hard, nonstip and bring my money home to my mate and treat her like the lady she is sweetheart. I can't help it this perfume of yours is fantastic . Usually perfume never affects me but this is yours and it has me really stirred up but I guess it's just because it's yours. You have such a sweet face and are as shapely a lady as I've ever seen and I truly want the honor to know you and want you as my fiance, so I guess your scent is mine now. It is beautiful here . We don't get the same weather that they do on the mainland as Cape Cod is 72 miles out in the ocean with sweet clean air. It looks alot like the Florida west coast around Sarasota, North Port except no palm trees. I love shopping ets and so we'll keep doing it if we ever get together. I hope so but if you can't hack it I understand but if you can honey you'll be a well cared for lasy as I am very affectionate , very loyal to my mate also I am passionate and you really appeal to me. I think you are a fine looking lady and I would hope you would let me love you in every way. I'm a one woman man who is tired of doing it all alone. You look like a very loving woman if your man treats you right. I sure will if you let me. I am a nice appearing man, clean neat and love nature and my lady. Won't you let me try to be your man?

Well , my sweet girl, I just can't take anymore of your sexy perfume right now as it is making me horney and no sense feeling that way with me here and you way down in Sarasota so I better close for now. My heart's door is open for you to come in if you want to. Please write me again soon and let me into your heart all the way. I'm putting your letter by my pillow so I can smell your lovely perfume and I can dream sweet dreams of love with you.

All my love to you,Roger, (MA.)

4-5-86

Dearest - My dearest Dorothy,

How are you this morning? I hope well and maybe thinking of me a little. I put your letter by my pillow and when I woke up that perfume of yours that drives me mad (a nice sweet man), was in my bed and I could almost feel you here beside me and I want to say hello, good morning and tell you I wish we were together right now, and I could show you just how your sweet pretty self and your tantalizing perfume affects me. I hope you use it on all your letters to me but not to anyone else. Perfume has always affected me but never like yours does. I just want you to know you are stealing my heart and I'm hoping you will just want it for your very own - and very soon too my darling. It's a beautiful day, a little cool but it's early yeat only 7 a.m.. The sky is clear blue no clouds the sun is shining brightly and I had to say good morning and let you know you are always on my mind. I keep your little picture from the album right with me and you are so cute and pretty. I'd like to reach out and hug and kiss you. I can't help it honey, that's how I feel and I am always honest.

The P.O. closes early so I will run over and see if maybe I have a letter from you though I'm sure I don't , too early, smile. I'm going to my favorite beach to feed my seagull friends. I always park and feed them at the same spot so when I park they are all there, sometimes over a hundred of them. They fill the sky as they are waiting for me to feed them. One of the markets in town sells day old bread and especially in the winter when fish are hard to get I bring them 20 to 30 big loaves for them to eat. They gather around me like children. They follow me along the beach like little puppy dogs and come when I call them. I've named one of them Charlie cause he comes out of the crowd to visit me. They are my friends here of course they always repay me kindness with their crapping on my windshield but so far they haven't christened me yet.

Well dear heart as I said this is just a note to tell you I am thinking about you and I hope to hear from you soon. Your letter is above my writing surface and the breeze from my window keeps b lowing your perfume right at me and makes me want to hug and kiss you and all the other sweet and gentle things I'd love to do with you.

Take care and take all my Love,Roger (MA.)

5-8-86

dear dorthy

got your name and photo from photo alburm club like what they said about you i am retired live alone wt one forty black hair brown eyes irish and indian dont drink or use drugs re tired painter have livable income dress well go glean have no chilren live in nice apt all my my self dont like to live alone have good car like to go to church i am a good man never ben in jail if you havent found the man of your dreams would like to hear from will send you my photo if you answer sincerely yours, loveWh (AR.)

5-19-86

Mrs. Dorothy Zimmerman

Dear Madam:

I took your name and address from a club magazine that I belong to and am writing to see if you would care to correspond if so I would like to hear from you all about your likes and dislikes and would like a picture of you if you would care to send it and I will answer and send you one of me if you would care to have it.

Thanks,D.D. (MD.)

7-25-86

Hello:

This is N.E. Fla #5546G of the Globe. Thank you very much for answering my add. I received many replys to that add and can't answer each one personally. Hope you understand. I do wish you much luck in finding a suitable partner.

Sincerely,#5546G (FL.)

8-17-86

Dear Dorothy,

Your name from Queens photo album. I am a male 68 good health work every day around here and help other people. I like to do things repair out doors. I like seeing things going places not alone no fun. I like fishing gardening almost anything outdoors. 5' 7 and a half", 196 Blue eyes Grey hair ruddy complexion. I am of good nature and easy to get alone with. Hamve home and car. I have been married 2 x's First one no good second one wonderful. Together for 14 years, cancer, heartsick 4 and a half years gone 6 years now. I am sitting at picnic table trying to write under maple tree very nice here. I don't have long hair and a beard. I'm clean don't drink smoke or dope. I would like very much to hear from you if you care to write.

Thank you,Nelson (MI.)

8-14-86

Dear Dot,

Hi! Done talking nothing else to say - only meet over a cup of coffee and see how we fit.

Take care, RegardsDon, (FL.)

Don also enclosed his calling card with his phone # and it says "No Job, No Money, No Ambition, No Home" which makes his quite irresistible wouldn't you say?

2-1-86

Hiya Dorothy,

I just got your resume thru Len's Club and it says you like to travel the beach. You are my kind of gal. Although I live on the opposite side of the world I too go to the Pacific beach which is a quarter mile from my home everyday weather permitting. I comb the beach 2 or 3 miles. I love it. I am also an artist I have sold many paintings. Gave away many to my family and friendsw. I also love to snap pictures of the beach the ocean and the sky. My favorites are the sunsets, Fantastic. What else do you do that I like to do? Do you like to snuggle are you affectionate? Do you swim why do you like the beach? I comb the beach I find petrified wood occassionally. I find an unusual stone of some kind. But with me I like to be there all the time if I could. I think you and I could wrestle pretty good. I'm with you my church is the beach. I have had prayers answered on the beach. My grandpappy always said the beach is as close to heaven as you will get. Here on the beach we could live on the beach. Anyway Dotty I don't know whether I told you or not I am 6 ' 200 lbs exmarine. I try to stay in shape. I exercise I love to walk. I am very easy to get alone with. I have blue eyes and white hair since I was thrity five and I am retired living on Social Security and a small pension from the marine corpse. I live in a trailer 10 x 60 , dress well, drive a nice car am comfortable. I think you and I will have alot of fun.

Sincerely yours, I am yours till Niagara Falls,LoveOllie, (CA.)

3-26-87

Dear Dottie,

I saw your nice as . I'm age 73 ,Ht. 6' , weight 175 brown eyes, grayish hair. I'm French all the way. I have a phone (Phone # enclosed) if near by give me a ring.

Sincerely,Wilburt, (NJ.)

Highly unlikely since she lives in Florida.

Dottie Zimmerman

5-14-87
Dear Dottie,
Enjoyed our phone conversation but a bit late in writing. I gave it much thought and feel that we have an age difference of 8 years. I know it's just a number but I feel that I should seek someone a little younger. Rather than disappoint you by not writing I did the honest thing. I answered as I promised. I didn't see any reason to enclose my snap. Keep well and best wishes.

p.s. I suppose your curious so I enclosed it anyhow!
best wishes,Richard, (FL.)

6-14-87
Hi Classie Lady:
Well, do you believe in the Easter Bunny or Santa Claus? Well, thats what you have here, but I also believe in God and the King James Bible. I am not a Jesus freak but try to get to church, if the fish aren't bite 'n. I don't smoke but may be considered to laughs over social drinking, twice a month or so. Gave up drugs for life and happyness some time ago with the California experience.

Well! if this hasn't scared you off yet, then let me go on, Ha! Ha!...My thing is travel, Motorcycle, car, R.V., boat, trailer, motel or hotel. Besides 14 times through out the U.S.A. I have been around the world three times from Alaska to New Zeland. I love going and doing but also like the idea of being able to stop without having to rush back to work.

I spent 6 years in the Navy with the Seals, aboard the U.S.S. Beamerton, Heavy Cruser (Show Boat of the Pacific Fleet) and at the same time kept up with my physical condition by studing the marshal arts (fifth degree Tie-kwan-doe and Mastered in Judo and SuVaute). I have lived a hard fast life, and have belonged to several major outlaw motorcycle gangs in California, after trying to be a Hippy in the sixties. I was raised with Sasquash in the mountains of Oregon, Washington, Idaho and Northern California until I was 18 years old. After the navy and four years as a outlaw biker I returned to my mountains. But I kept drifting towards the beaches (don't get me wrong, beaches is spelled correctly) more and more until I could stand it no longer. I joined the Merchant marines to see the world again .

What? Your still reading! As you probly have guessed I am a twenty

106

five year old, trapped in a 47 year old body and if we are worried about age then we are in trouble already. My hair is turning silver but I can still dance until morning. My belly is more on the teddy bear side now (table muscle), but it is water and sodas because I don't like beer that much. I only drink to be one of the boys, if you know what I mean. I realize this doesn't give you much to go on but I am shy and have never tryed this type of correspondence before so please bare with me.

Yes, I am 47 years old and a Leo, with a Gemini rising sign with Mercury moon a risin. I love travel, movies, travel, window shopping, camping, dinning, dancing, fishing, exploring, bible studys and don't forget going places, Ha! Ha! Six foot zero and a half ince, silver brown hair just past my sholders..ahhhhhhhh, six inches past? Oh well, I am two hundred and eighty pounds and they don't mistake me as a lady Ha! Ha! Especially with my beard, which is shaved off my neck and under my lover lip like Kenney Rodgers but whiter more like Willy Nelson. I have been mistaken for Marlon Brando while in California and Willy Nelson quite often, whish I had their money!

Still with me? Boy, your a glutton for punishment. Well what do you think? Ready for the bad things? Says the grasshopper to the ant, I have been playing all my life and now I just don't seam to make enough money to travel anymore. Someones always got his hand out. Fix car, pay rent and ect. I would like a grasshopper to share my life with, my expertice in the great outdoors and my world travels. To quote something my daddy use to say, "Man, with sense and no dollars, looking for lady with no sense and dollars." I am just joking, with four years at Los Angeles Trade Tech College in Los Angeles, California and six years at Clark College in Vancouver, Wash., I would at least like communicate with my future helpmate.

I am a jack of all trades. I work on the restoration of trailers, R.V.'s , cars and homes. I am concidered a pretty good intereator decerator and injoy working on lan d scapes including my own. Wrting is something I really injoy but can't afford, as is the case of my second love...computers. It seamses that the landlord wants his money every time you turn around and if I do finally save a couple of dollars I take off to Disney World, Epcot center in Florida, Disneyland in California, and Caverns for the beauty as like Cypress Gardens in Florida, Key West or just anywhere, in the world. And now with France and England building more Disney complexes.........?

I don't want to be somebodies house boy but a shoulder? A friend? A companion? A helpmate, Yes! Close for now, waiting for your picture and comments. My sister is making some of me. They won't scare you I promise! You have any snap shots in swim wear?

With all my love your friend,Robbin (FL.)

2-15-86

Dear Dorothy

I got your resume from Maurines list I thought I would drop you a line to ask you if you cared to correspond with me. I will try to tell you something of myself. I am 6' , 200 lbs., exmarine. I exercise and walk on our beach here on the Pacific. I love to beachcomb . I find many pc's of debris or bric a brac that has been made into something else. I love nature I am am a painter or was until my wife died. My desire to paint seemed to die with her. I raised 5 kids all married and on their own now. I live alone in a trailer 10' by 60'. I substituted a disc camera instead of paint brush an d it takes wonderful photos. I walk the beach everyday weather permitting. I dress well drive a nice car . I am comfortable except for medication for a little high blood pressure . I just had a cataract removal and a lens implant. I can see wonderful only one eye, the other was near perfect. 72 years young Mar 27-1914. Anything else you want to know just ask.

Sincerely yours until the apples turn over,Oliver,(OR.)

2-23-86

Dear Dorothy,

What part of Phila. did you live in? I lived in the northeast in Frankford and I worked for the Phila. gas co. for 12 years as a C.S. man and a salesman and a appliance installer. As a matter of fact I have two daughters and a son living in northeast Philly now as I probably didn't tell you my wife and I raised 5 kids which are all wed and on their own. We lived in El Cajou Cal for 15 yrs. we had a small ranch there but it was like a zoo. We had all kinds of animals 6 or 7 horses, birds of all kinds doves. We had what is called a mundane pidgeon it gets so big like 10 to 12 pounds. it can't get airborne, too heave, . We had peacocks, donkeys, goats, it kept me broke trying to feed them all. But takes water and utilities took whatever you had left. And you couldn't tell whether it was Dec. or June,But up here in Ore. along the coast no snow no cold , winters are mild and we stay greener than Cal. because usually we get more rain than Cal. Also in our area we are too high to flood so you see we are near Utopia. Last month our fruit trees are blooming and alla the smaller flowers are in bloom. Where else does trees or plants bloom in Feb.. I live about a quarter mile from the Pafcific beach. I love to comb it for two or three miles when the wheather permits. Some people say folks from Ore, don't die they rust away. I'm sorry I don't have a painting to send you what I haven't sold the kids fight over. Tell you what I took photos of some of the paintings I sold I am keeping for reference because I have stopped painting since my wife died 8 yrs. ago. I'll send them to you to see if you'll send them back to me. I am 6' 200 lbs. exmarine I try to keep in shape. I love our beach too, I am Irish and Chickasaw Indian. My grandpappy use to guide folks across country to Ore. He looked just like sitting bull. I always said there is no house in the world big enough for two women. I feel sorry for you. Please send the photos back not me the others.

Sincerely yours Dorothy, yours till Niagara FallsOliver,(OR.)

5-11-88

Dear Mrs. or Ms.,

I read your letter ad in the Globe it sounds good to me. I am a widower , 79, 5' 11", 182 . I am marriage minded. I'm retired on Social Security and State Retirement. My father people English , my mother Holland Dutch. I live in 3 room apt . in a senior bldg. it pretty good but living alone in it not the greatest thing. It hard to write the first letter. I don't know to tell you. I hope you don't mind or they say I will make this letter short and sweet. I hope I hear from you . If you care to call me I will take care of the call. (phone # inserted)

Yours truely,Courtland, (MA.)

5-11-88

Dear Pretty Lady,

Maybe some day we might meet. I am an 84 year old man. I feel like a drowning man who grasps for a straw but I am honest and sincere person. I am in fairly good health. I don't smoke or use tobacco in any form. I don't drink any liquor nor use any kind of drugs.

Financially I have not too much. I have a pension and Social Security that gives me $850.00 a month and 10 nthousand in savings. A new car a

Chrvrolet Cavalier 1987, all paid for. I live in a retired complex 51 apartments so have to relocate.

I can't live through another winter in Mich. . I have a son 60 yrs. old retired and going to live in Florida. I have a daughter who is retiring Aug. 1st., her husband just took early retirement May 1st.. My family will never be any problems for me.

I have lived here 3 years but I have to go to a warmer climate. I have spent 12 winters in Florida. We had an older mobile home in a Zephyrhills mobile park. I sold it 2 years ago. We have been to many places in Florida so Florida is not new to me.

I am 5 ' 10 " tall and weigh 145 lbs.. I can do some cooking and have done apt. cleaning and go to a laundromat to do my washing. My last wife divorced me and just about cleaned me out. We were married 20 months. She got an 85 Chevrolet a 25 inch T.V. a clothes dryer. I finished paying for a new electric cook stove and a lawn mower. I had a savings of $10,400.00 in a joing account and she drawed it out and put in her name so I am quite bitter but I hate no one. I am just hoping I can find someone that we can live together love each other and have the rest of lives together and be happy.

Love,Albert , (MI.)

5-13-88
Hello 91901,
My name is Bill. I am 6' 2" around 260 lbs. born 4, black hair, hazel eyes. I am now retired as of 4-27. I came here from St. Pete, Fl. and I now live near Macclen , just signed a contract for a few acres out of town. I have 2 horses . I use to rodeo for about 18 years. I love fishing, camping and cooking the fish right there. With slice tom. and yr. I'll bet you are a good cook. I wood like to meet you. I look 20 years younger than my age. Do you like to fish , camp out? Phone # (inserted)
Bill, (FL.)

Next comes a Christmas card with a note dated:

12-12-88
Honey
I'll sure miss your picture. It just kept me warm all the time. I sure wish we could have been together but I guess we were too far apart. I'll

just bet we would have been good together. I have thought about you alot. I sure hope that everything that is good comes to you. You just might write if you want to:

Your hidden lover,Virgilxxxxxxx , (IN.)

5-12-88

Dearest Friend.

A short letter for and introduction in response to your ad in the Sheela Wood section..

A tall nice looking fellow 6' 3", dark hair w gray. Slim built sincere, affectionate, caring understanding and dependable. Enjoy busy mornings afternoon walks, antiques, traveling sightseeing and the Catskill Mountains some in New York. Perhaps we could meet and see if the chemistry is right. One never knows until one sees. Will give more information at meeting time as by phone which is (phone#).

Cheers,Don,(NY.)

6-20-88

Dearest Dottie,

Received your letter with your photo. I must say your one attractive lady for your age. Delighted to hear from you and to have your photo.

We are extremely compatible in so many ways. We like the same things. Think alike in many ways like nice things. Romantic love to be touched and carressed "Wow!" so much for that. Here is a photo of this old boy himself. It will give you an idea of what I look like . Hope you like it. Was taken 2 years ago. It is very hot here 80 90 degrees weather. I guess you are use to the hot weather after living in Florida. Do hope to hear from you.

Take care, Sincerely,Don, (NY.)

This next one is a christmas card with an enclosed short note.

12-20-88

Dear Dottie,

Recived your add in friendly singles I like your add and your age . will write a few lines and tell you a little about myself I am 5 ft. 7 inches wet 145 pounds brown eyes , hair is turning. Don't drink or smoke. I fishing camping and play a little on the guitar c & w music . My name is

Florenzo. If interested please write soon.

  Florenzo, (IL.)

  8-4-89

  Dear Dottie,

  I will try and get a letter to you. You say you are 75 ,5 and 7 , . I am 5 7 and one half tall and wt 100 and 60 lbs. age 80. You can write me if you get this letter. I sure hope you get my letter. You did not say what town you live in. I sure would like to hear from you.

  Fred,(KA.)

  1-7-90

  Dear 448FL. Dottie Zimmerman,

  I'm not sure whether I qualify, according to your specifications, but I'll let you be the judge. I am a SWM, 80 never married. 5' 6 and a half", 145#, healthy, non drinker or smoker. I am an ex Lutheran .

  Just completed 3 yrs plus as a volunteer at R.C. and Manatee Hospital in the Emergency Care Center. I have two nieces in Bradenton . They are the reason I came here from Oregon. I am neither rich or broke, just comfortable . I have no outstanding bills. Live alone in a mobile home in my trailer park (Address inserted). I agree with you as to your likes to do. I will add I love to read, write, meet people , attend lectures. My life has been material for a book.

  I am not familiar with Sarasota, so I will not drop in on you unless invited. We could if you like talk by phone. My number is (phone # inserted). Would you like a photo of me? What I really would like to do is to retire. Find a better half who can put up with me. Get married and live a life that is safe and sane. And let the rest of the world let me overcome lonliness.

  It would be nice, if we could start corresponding and let the future take care of itself.

  Hope I hear from you soon,Harold (FL.)

About the Author

As I rapidly approach the threshold of my 90th birthday, I still hold onto an illusion of yet another wedding day. I must be insane since even after this twenty year dry spell I have once again joined a singles club. If Oprah and Donohue both endorse it, I figure it can't be all bad, Ha! Ha!

Being this old I've lived through a lot of history. From Orson Well's panic evoking radio broadcast of *War of the Worlds* right up to the shock of 9/11's terrible Tuesday, the worst yet. I felt that methods of courting are also of historic value in their own simple way. After thinking about it that way I also felt this accumulation of painstakingly collected correspondence might be of value as some extremely interesting reading material. People might want to read about twenty years of unrequited love letters. You know a basic educational guide on how not to do it seemed worthy of documentation. So, this is my one and only contribution to the literary world. Hey, if it was good enough for Grandma Moses, what the hell!

www.ingramcontent.com/pod-product-compliance
Lightning Source LLC
Chambersburg PA
CBHW030341290526
45785CB00004B/1555